Going Through the Door and
FINDING MIRACLES:
A Warts and All Testimony

Janice Rae Sanders

E xulon ELITE

This book is dedicated to…
My brother Ronnie…
I will miss you every day until God reunites us.
I know you ARE with Jesus.

And…

My sister Lori…whom I always have loved,
and who has always loved me.
Thank you Jesus for forgiveness.

Quick Words from the Author

I did my best to put myself out there, without invading the privacy of others. My dates may be a little off, but I have tried my best to put the moments in the correct time period. I have broken most of God's commandments, and it does no good to give details about affairs I have had. It is not my wish to hurt others. However, I will give you this...not enough to get me into the Guinness Book of World Records. I have always known Jesus was Lord, and never dabbled with religions. I knew he was IT, but gave nothing to him, and yet he loved me.

If this book reaches one person who is troubled, or searching for God, and if it results in one baptism in Jesus' name, I will consider it a huge success. Feel free to send comments to <u>janicesanders@ earthlink.net</u>. Thank you.

Janice Rae Sanders

Special Thanks

All Praise and Glory to my Savior Jesus.

And in no particular order...

Jake...I couldn't have done this without you...I lived it, wrote it, and you waded through more than 40,000 words to help me present it. Your dedication to the Chosen one and I brings such warmth to my heart, and you are family.

Michael...I told you it was not my intent to embarrass anyone in our family, and you replied, "Mom, you are years too late for that." You never knew what a time out was, but you knew what respect was. How you make me smile!

Rudy...I never cut the cord with you boys, because I never wanted to. Thank you for being the keeper of those early memories.

Tiffany...as long as I have breath in my body, I will be there for you. Thank you for all the joy you have given me.

Rudy's Father...who taught me patience, and a love of Christmas.

Michael's Father...who rescued me, and gave me a strong sense of family.

Gene's Sons...you gave me a chance, and I love you both.

Verna...my dear friend, may I live to see you baptized.

Nancy...different paths, but we always can make each other laugh, sooooo "Red Rover, Red Rover......let Nancy come over!"

Rose...we are the last of the three Musketeers...thank you for loving me, even if you don't see me.

Pete...I wish I had a dollar for every time I said, "What would I do without Pete."

Michelle...you are number one with me, and you truly are a good person.

Mrs. Foster...my lifeline, my phone a friend, my sponsor that strengthens my Faith.

Brother Chris...who prayed for me and stood beside me when I first received the Holy Spirit, the gift of speaking in tongues.

Justin...my neighbor, though you moved 6 miles away now, I know you are always there for me.

Liz...the most "down to earth" big shot I have ever met, and who is my uplifting cheerleader!

Sherry...you planted the seed.

Mike and Cheryl...who are old school, and never forgot where they came from, I owe you both so much.

Larry and Tim...every time I hear the word integrity, you both flash into my mind...any time I want to debate, I know you both will rise to the challenge

CCPD of the past, Wally, Don, Danny, Bobby, Al and all the rest of you that fought against corruption...I was proud to know, and stand with you during those difficult days.

My husband Gene...who has never tried to stop me from being me, and has deepened my Faith, without knowing it.

My Pastor Jason Cox and his wife Sister Alyssa, and my Church Steger Apostolic...when I walk through the doors I am at home. Thank you for your tireless efforts to bring us HIS WORD, and guide us through your examples of what we strive to be.

My birth mother Rae Jane...thank you for letting me enter this world.

Ron...thank you for being my friend in this game of life.

My mom, GG...you went through the door God put in front of you. Thank you Mom for loving me.

You the reader...my hope is that this book will let you know you are not alone. That you will realize everyone has a past, and it is not how you entered this world, but how you leave it. May this book give you courage to take those steps towards finding Jesus. That is the only "royalty" I seek...that you accept Him.

Introduction

B efore I became a born again Christian, I always felt different, like I had some sort of purpose...not like I was better than others, or all that...just different.

I thought a lot about "why I was here?" I was just a kid, maybe 12 or so, but I used to think "why me?"

There are people that are kind of "lukewarm Christians" I don't think I was even that high up on the faith leader board. My standard answer about my faith was "hey, I'm no Mother Teresa, but I ain't Richard Speck either." That kind of encompassed my belief. I believed in God, but wondered, why me, why did I get chosen to walk the earth, I mean, I liked myself, but as a freckled red head kid, I thought of myself as mediocre. Not the cheer leader, not the prom queen, not the kid that got bullied every day, but just someone moving in the halls at school. But yet, I felt different...but I didn't dwell on that too long...there was too much going on in life, the 50s the 60s (oh those 60s) and the 70s and 80s etc. I did love the time period I was born into.

Anyway, miracles started showing up in my life early on, but I didn't recognize them...in fact if they manifested themselves in the 60's well, they were lost in a "tune in, turn on, drop out" phase of my life. Looking back, I think the earliest miracle that I remember about myself, happening to me...was when I tried to teach myself how to swim. Wolf Lake was pretty treacherous, and lots of kids drown there...but was I thinking about that, nope. I was with a few friends and I was in chest deep water, when I decided to teach myself to swim...now most people would start doggy paddling TOWARDS SHORE, but not little Janney...I started doggy paddling all I was worth, towards the horizon, looking across the water. I wanted to see, how far I got, so I stopped...and you guessed it, was in deep water...I flailed around, but mostly sank like a stone, and didn't have time to yell out. A friend of mine was on shore, and he saw me, and didn't think much, when he suddenly remembered I couldn't swim. Here is what I do remember...I wasn't scared, it was really peaceful, almost like I saw myself floating downwards under the water in a giant soap bubble. I woke up on shore, I guess my friend grabbed me, by the hair, and took me to shore and I remember lying flat on the ground and coughing and people all around. But I am telling you, while I was drowning, I was at peace.

Now I wish I could remember all my miracles in the correct order, but since I am no spring chicken, I am going to just have to write them down as they come to me. Thank you Jesus, for not letting me die that day.

I rarely thanked Jesus or God for anything in those years, sadly, a lot of years, where I believed in God, but didn't want to be bothered to attend boring church. I would much rather stay up late watching Shock Theater...

Saturday monster movies...My parents, (though we lived next to the minister) didn't attend church much, though Mom did a stint, singing in the choir...so it was hard to pressure my brother and I into going. Though, they did try the old...don't do as I do, do as I say number.

It's funny, but now I thank God every day, and I ask forgiveness too, and I still mess up tons, and I don't know if I will ever be good enough, in fact, is anyone ever good enough to deserve the sacrifices Jesus made for us. No...but again, I will still feel less deserving than others that I perceive to be better church members and better Christians.

I don't want to jump too far ahead, and some miracles are really mind blowing, while others are kind of subtle... but I am sharing them all, and you can pick and choose what ones you like, if any.

I do know this...people talk about intuition, and gut feelings...THIS I HAVE LEARNED...that voice inside of you, the one that tells you what not to do, or gives you a nudge to do the right thing (and we rarely listen) well folks, that is GOD TALKING TO US...it is, and the funny thing is that when you listen to it, it never steers you wrong. I mean most of the time, you just want to do what you want to do, and so we ignore him. But I have found that every time I have listened to it, it has benefited me tremendously and saved my life several times.

Like the time I was driving to work, down our block on 156th street, in Cal City. A typical side street (we lived next to a tavern) and so our street was one way and I had to drive down the block, turn at the corner, and stop at a stop sign and turn right to get to the main road. I had the radio blaring, as usual, and I did a cursory stop at the stop sign, a rolling stop, and started forward, when the voice inside me yelled STOP! It yelled so loud inside me that I DID STOP. And it's a good thing I did, because a car doing about 60 flew by me and would have broadsided me right in my door...I am sure I would have died that day. The music was loud, and cars that are traveling at a high rate of speed, usually appear out of nowhere. It shook me up, I mean, that car didn't even slow, and who barrels down side streets like that anyway. But that was a life changing moment...I lived. I didn't give any credit, where credit was due...just thought I was lucky, and that my intuition kicked in. I actually tried not to think too much about it, as it made me sick to my stomach. I had two young sons, and a husband, and I wasn't thinking about dying, or living...just about getting to work on time.

Table of Contents

Chapter 1:

My Early Life

My early life was not the life of the Cleavers, or the Brady Bunch kids. My birth mother, committed suicide...hanging herself by my crib. I found out when I was walking to school...a group of older kids enlightened me...I was five.

When I asked the questions, as to why, (I didn't ask till I was about 12) I was told she had the Baby Blues, and I was 6 months old when it happened. However, I saw one of those religious cards they give you at funerals, and I was more like two when she did it. So I think we can rule out post-partum depression.

My father never said much, just "You have a mother now, so leave it alone." My Dad remarried when I was almost six.

My Dad said that when he dated, and he got around to mentioning he had two motherless children at home, the lady would excuse herself to use the restroom, and sneak out of the restaurant. He dated a woman named Marilyn for a while, and I liked her, she gave me underwear with the different days of the week on them. I was not thrilled when I met Carallee. I lived with my Aunt Elsie, and only saw my father on weekends. Those early years with Aunt Elsie were not easy, and I loved her and Uncle Wilbur with all my heart. My brother was in a home for boys for a while, but ran away when they beat him for not eating his oatmeal. He stayed four blocks away at Aunt Maydees. It might as well have been four miles...I was a little kid, and I wasn't even allowed to cross the street, let alone travel to 106th street.

I had to leave Aunt Elsie's for a time. I used to sit on Uncle Wilbur's lap, what he had of a lap anyway, as he was overweight, and I would have my little cowboys from the Fort Apache set march up his stomach and chest like they were scaling a mountain. I liked the smell of his pipe, and loved the ritual of watching him clean and fill the pipe. He always dozed, or so I thought while I sat on his lap. I vaguely remember, Aunt Elsie walking in, and yelling "Wilbur" and it was because my dear old Uncle had unzipped his fly, and had himself exposed, feinting sleep, and hoping little Janice would touch him. So I was shipped off, and stayed at some ladies house, but I came down with pneumonia, and ended up in the hospital. I still remember that the first night in the hospital was the longest night of my life...I didn't sleep. I lay awake for hours and was pretty miserable. I also hated the bedpan. It was in the hospital that I learned to become an activist. I was in a large ward of children. One of the nurses was a cruel, cruel woman, and she had red hair. She would pull our hair, and hit us with the hairbrush. She threatened all of us...she said we'd never see our families again if we told. She slapped us too. Lots of the kids cried, and after one such torturous shift, I became the Union leader. I took our grievances to my father! My father visited everyday on his lunch hour…and when I told him, he went crazy.

My kind father, the guy who made me laugh every day, while wearing a Donald Duck puppet on his hand… ran out of there like his hair was on fire. He grabbed the first nurse he saw, and asked if it was this one…and it wasn't. Anyway, needless to say, the nurse was fired…it turned out that she was recently released from a mental hospital or something like that. I guess they didn't do background checks in the 50s. So I went back to Aunt Elsie's, but they kept Uncle Wilbur far away from me. The incident was never mentioned to me, and I recalled all of it the day I walked into a tobacco store and smelled the pipe tobaccos.

Okay, so back to meeting my mother…except she wasn't my new mother yet…it was a date…a meet the kids date. Now, Carallee was from the Cayman Islands. For years kids thought I said the Grand Canyon, and they had no idea where this place was. The children in the Caymans were raised to respect adults, everything was yes ma'am, and yes sir etc. And the Cayman people did not spare the rod and spoil the child, though the only thing they revered more than their children was God.

Imagine poor Carallee's shock at my first words to her. "Who is she?" "Why does SHE have to go with us?" "I don't want her to come with to the museum with us!" Just so you don't think I was a total brat, remember I only saw my father and brother on weekends. Just when I thought I was getting somewhere, and maybe, she was not going with, she takes me by the arm and announces she is going to give me a BATH!!!!! I WAS HORRIFIED. Sure I had dirty sweat streaks on my arms, but you get those when you are digging a hole to China. I waited for my father to intervene, and he just pretended to be busy with something else. She actually had to drag me, my shoes scraping the toes on the sidewalk, as I was having none of this, and I never did admit the bath was refreshing.

I did get even though. I planted myself between the two front seats. This was in the days of no seat belts, and I stood on that little hump on the floor in the back seat, and wedged myself between them both, talking a mile a minute so they couldn't get a word in edgewise. My beloved brother Ronnie, whom I adored,

had the audacity to tell me he actually liked this woman! I was not to be won over, and I carried a grudge the rest of the week.

Now, for the lesson learned here, and this is important! GOD OPENS MANY DOORS FOR US... WE CAN CHOOSE TO WALK THROUGH THEM, OR TO SLAM THEM SHUT. THANK YOU JESUS THAT CARALLEE JACKSON FROM SAVANNAH, GRAND CAYMAN, WALKED THROUGH THAT DOOR. It changed my life forever. But of course I didn't realize how much, until much later in life. But let's fast forward to more miracles.

Rae Jane my birth mother

Ron and I-picture taken at the time I
was living with Aunt Elsie

10 year old me with Mom and Dad with Lori
on the way

Chapter 2:

Young and Dumb

My brother Ronnie bought a 327 Biscayne Chevy. It was black with red interior. He was 18 at the time, and I was 14.

Those were the days when teens drag raced every light when there wasn't a cop in sight. Ronnie and his girlfriend Carol (later to become his wife) and my brother's friends would pile in the car and go cruising.

As a kid, I was wild to tag along. Remember Mackenzie Phillips in American Graffiti? That gangly, homely kid? That was me! Every so often Ronnie would take me joy riding. I would have turned down a plane trip to Hawaii to get the chance to ride shotgun with my brother at the wheel.

Ron's car was fast, and he won quite often. I was with him and the guys (no shotgun for the kid, just wedged in the back seat) when a convertible full of guys pulled up alongside of us, gunning their motor. Both drivers were appraising the other's ride, and the driver of the convertible threw down a bet...Ronnie being the wise guy said he'd bet his sister! ME??? Yup, my brother bet me. He was joking and knew he would win, but still!!! The other driver said ok, and we took off. We weren't on any straight away; we were on side roads in a neighborhood near Whiting, Indiana.

It was pretty exhilarating, and Ron won easily. He turned to the guy and said, "Well you lost, so pay up, and you can still have my sister." WHAT?! I WAS HUMILIATED, AND I WAS GONNA SHOW MY BROTHER UP! Before Ron knew what was happening, I jumped out of that car, and hopped in the convertible!!! Take that Mr. Loudmouth! But...OH NO, THE CONVERTIBLE TOOK OFF WITH ME AT A HIGH RATE OF SPEED! I didn't plan for this to happen; I wasn't even wearing a seatbelt. I yelled stop, but those guys were having none of it and flew down the streets with Ronnie in hot pursuit. We took a corner way too fast and started spinning, landing on someone's lawn, almost hitting the front porch...dirt and grass and smoke flying everywhere! Ron and the guys jumped out of the Chevy and were next to us in seconds it seemed. The driver of the convertible and everyone else was to shaken to stand. Ronnie gestured with his thumb and said four words to me, "GET IN THE CAR!"

Later, upon reflection, I was glad he didn't add idiot to the end of the sentence. My legs were rubber and I had a hard time getting out of the car, and I was walking like I had too much to drink. When Ron got behind the wheel again, he said five more words to me, "Did you learn a lesson?" I still couldn't talk and just nodded. He looked so angry. Even if I could have come up with a smart aleck remark, I wouldn't have the nerve to say it.

Yes he was foolhardy and so was I. He was 18 and I was 14. Young and dumb. That was true in the 60s and still is today so often, when you read a sad story and just shake your head...what were those kids thinking? God was there that day...he got us all out of that mess. Please, please pray over your children before they go out the door and ask the Lord to surround them with protection.

After looking at this picture I can see
why my brother gave me away

Chapter 3:

Rudy

always wanted children, and I had the perfect scenario
in my mind...I'm married to a loving husband, I am
schooled in the artistry of cooking, (think Betty Crocker
here) and I have six lovely children. Ahhh pipe dreams.
I was madly, obsessively in love, and I got pregnant.
He was in the Army at the time. An abortion was suggested. Abortions were performed in New York at the
time, and a friend of the child's father (in the day I would
have said fetus, but now I say child) offered to go with
me to New York and pay for the abortion. He was sin-
cerely trying to help me, as the love of my life did not
want any obligations. I was worried and I thought about
it, but then a thought came to me, like a little voice inside.
"If you are not on my side, then who is? Then I have no
one." It was like the baby was talking to me. I decided
against the abortion and decided to end my relationship
too, and go it alone.

I waited for the phone call from the Army base, and
I told him it was over. He told me he was coming home,

he actually went AWOL and I think he had some help there, as he was never caught. He proposed to me and we married.

Fast forward to the birth...I had never anticipated birth to be this way. I had heard all the horror stories and I was already on edge. My doctor had estimated the delivery date to be Halloween, and now it was December 10th and the baby was finally on the way. Labor started around noon, so I figured a baby by 3 or 4.

I had never heard of birth classes, learning how to breathe with the pain. The hospital was jammed and every woman seemed to be trying to have her child before Christmas. On the way to the hospital my husband argued with me that he wanted to name the child Eli if it was a boy. I wanted the name Rudy. After the first 15 hours of torture, he looked at me and said "you can name the baby whatever you want" he was in tears and I wanted to just die from the pain. Rudy finally came into the world after 26 hours of labor. I was so out of it, I didn't even know I had a baby.

My first thought when I held him, was that I would worry about him for the rest of my life. I was spot on with that revelation. Rudy was the most perfect child. Handsome like his father, none of my freckles (hooray) and was such an easy baby, and I was filled with all the wonder and love that your first child brings.

If I could have I would have sealed him up in a protective bubble. I wanted to keep him safe and protected. Did you ever know of anyone that had emergency tracheotomy instructions (using an eyedropper) taped on the refrigerator? I did.

What an amazing child Rudy was, or should I say Rudolph, as that was his official name. He didn't run and scream like most little children, he was in awe of everything the world held for him. He had such an intent look on his face, whether he was looking at the sky, or reading a book. He learned to read at the age of 3, not memorize, but read. Ironically, now he never picks up a book, but as a child he loved the library. We talked about all the important things he should know: butterflies, clouds, Christmas, and occasionally Jesus. I warned him about every danger out there. He never, ever, disregarded my words about safety. Never tried to cross the street alone, or played with matches. He knew what "stranger danger" was. He had firsthand knowledge of that. When he was five, walking to kindergarten with his friend, a man accosted them. He hit Rudy from behind knocking him down and grabbing the friend, trying to run off with them. The boys fought, and he dropped the child. The police were called, I couldn't wait for that, I went to every house, every apartment in the area, and was given information to a man that matched the description. I gave my tips to the police, the man was picked up. Rudy identified the likeness of the man, and we never had to go to court. Apparently he was out on bail on unrelated charges, so he was sent away for a long time. I was glad the boys were spared the ordeal of court and trials.

I have a letter from my son that was written to me when my brother died. He didn't give it to me until I faced a medical crisis a few months later. It is one of my most precious possessions.

He is artistic, and thinks differently than the rest of the world. Everyone wants to be his friend. I like to think that he got the very best that his father and I had to give. He also saved my life. This child that I considered not having, saved my life. As I said before the doctor calculated his birth to be Halloween. The pregnancy was difficult, but we needed the money. I worked downtown and had an excellent job, and I was my boss' right hand, his confidant, and he put unbelievable faith and trust in me, and I was only 23. I have always felt that when you love what you do, it isn't work. I have felt that about every type of employment I have ever had, be it waitress, or secretary, I loved all my jobs.

Forgive my repeating myself, but I was very sick, but we needed the money, bottom line, and I struggled to work every day. I took the commuter train, and the smells of South Chicago played havoc with my nausea. I struggled each day, and finally I told my husband I just couldn't do it anymore. The baby was due Halloween, and so I quit work a couple of weeks early. Most women have morning sickness in only the first trimester. I was sick constantly, and if only it would have confided itself to mornings. It was going to be a struggle, but my husband understood. So about two weeks before Halloween I gave notice and was filled with the relief that I didn't have to travel to the Loop every day.

On October 30th, 1972 The Illinois Central Railroad had one of the worst train wrecks in Chicago's history. Forty five people were killed when one train slammed into another. I recognized several women in the photos that the newspaper ran. You see, we all always rode in the same railroad car! We would nod hello, sometimes remark about the weather, but we were ships that passed in the night. Many in that car were decapitated. If I had known my baby was not arriving until December, I would have forced myself to continue working and riding that train. My unborn son saved my life, he made me so ill I had to resign my place of employment, and he gave the appearance of arriving sooner than should be expected. My son's favorite holidays are Halloween and Christmas. He loved Halloween so much. I once had his birthday celebrated that day instead of December 11th. Death was waiting for a lot of people that day in October, but it was not in God's plan for me.

I know all my children's faults, and they know mine, and point them out occasionally...usually when I am lecturing them about something that's on my mind.

I believe that once you bring them into the world, your job doesn't end at 18. If you are 50 and I'm 80, and I think you are doing something wrong, I am going to bring it to your attention. I have been reminded before that they are full grown adults. I counter with, "I don't care how old you are, you will never be on my level! I am your mother, and until I die, I'm at the top rung of the ladder, in this family."

It's funny the things that you remember that touches your heart about your children. I remember walking across the parking lot at Home Depot, Rudy and I deep in conversation, and without losing a sentence, or stopping the conversation with me, he cuts across the parking lot to help a lady that couldn't get the shopping carts unstuck. He did it without any thought to doing it... another time I helped some young kid that was in trouble, I didn't know him, but that didn't matter.

The next morning I received a dozen roses from Rudy, the card read "I have never been so proud of you in my life Mom, I love you."

I hope this gives you a little overview of my witty, charismatic, handsome son, my firstborn Rudy.

Me sitting to cover the missing tiles

Rudy and Michael on the way to my brother's funeral

Rudy and Michael

Chapter 4:

Michael

Michael is my middle child, my second born, my baby, until we "got the girl" as I like to joke. Just as Rudy was like his father in so many ways…so is my son Michael like his father.

When I see him, I think "strength" he is stoic. When Michael calls me with a problem, he always starts the sentence with "I got this, so don't worry, I just wanted your input and opinion Mom." There are no gray areas with Michael. He is honest, and has a lot of integrity. He is a one woman man, not a player, and he is generous, but careful with his money. Michael respects women, and though he was a black belt in karate at the age of 12 (both my sons were) he is a gentle teddy bear, but don't try to play mind games or push his buttons. He is careful with investments, and as a Union man, he buys American. He has always excelled at sports, is a good dancer, and though he is the younger brother, he is second to no one. I can't use his emotions or love for me to convince him to buy into my way of thinking. He will only do so if he agrees with me. The argument never gets past "MA, NO...DON'T ASK ME TO DO THAT THE ANSWER IS NO" and he is always respectful while he is saying that. Michael has my eyes, and both my boys are 6'4" and handsome guys. If work is slow, or money is tight, you would never know it. He works through his problems, and on the few occasions he let me help, it was with much reluctance. He broke his arm, and hated watching me scrubbing his floors on my hands and knees, so he helped me with his one good arm.

My husband and I wanted another child, and I lost that baby to a miscarriage. I didn't realize I was pregnant again so soon, and Michael was an easy, no stress pregnancy. He was reluctant to come out and meet the world, so on May 10, 1977 my labor was induced and my 9 pound son was born. My husband was the last of his line and so when our Italian son was born, the family went crazy. His father came straight to the hospital, and thanked me for his grandson. My mother in law made me stuffed artichokes; I craved them while I was in labor. Our Aunts and Uncles called him Mikey, and dubbed him the "sacred cow" and whatever doubts my in-laws had about me (I wasn't Italian) vanished with the birth of this grandson.

Just as easy as Rudy was, Michael was like a Tasmanian devil. He was nicknamed Damien by his Aunt. He head butted out the bottom of his play pen, chewed his beautiful wooden crib to splinters, climbed on a counter and removed a sharp knife from the top shelf and sliced his leg open, requiring 8 stitches.

He got the cap that covered the bolts on the toilet stuck in his throat. When things were calm, Rudy did his best to help Michael liven things up. After watching Rocky, Rudy convinced him to jump from the top bunk bed onto a small Star Wars pillow. Michael broke his arm. Rudy took cookies out of the pantry and sprayed them with raid and hid them in our basement family room, hoping to catch ants. Michael ate all the cookies. Back to the hospital. He burned himself on the BBQ grill, and while rolling around on our shag carpet, got a penny stuck in his forehead, just above his eye. We were at the hospital so often that after a terrible reaction to a bug bite that swelled both his eyes shut, his father and I were questioned by the medical staff. We were vindicated when they found the bug bite among the swelling. Michael was all BOY!

We enrolled him in karate classes, and he was the Joe Frazier of the Karate school. He would advance forward, never backing up and then take out his opponent, 1 2 3. When he won the first, of his many first place trophies, I felt like my son took the gold medal at the Olympics. I still remember the summer his team took second place in their little league. We had a chance at first, but after walking several opposing players, our pitcher burst into tears and we took second place. Michael played catcher and was one of the "long ball hitters. I thought of their team as "The boys of summer" and that summer was golden.

We were never spare the rod or spoil the child type of parents. My reasoning is this…you can talk till you're blue in the face, they can listen, appear contrite, argue back, promise you the moon, but once they went out the door, you really never knew how it would go. Maybe they really were sorry for whatever it was they did to make you come down on them...or maybe, they laughed about it with their friends. I knew that if I smacked them, it got their attention. Whatever they were thinking before, they now noticed I was serious. As the boys got older, and stronger, and got into more trouble, I became more resourceful. I would grab a wooden spoon and go after those two 6'4" teens that decided they were men, and didn't need to follow my rules. It worked great for a while, I would chase and they would flee, until one day Michael stood his ground and faced me down, smiling. I went for him, and he disarmed me quicker than you can say "Karate Kid" and broke my good wooden spoon over his knee. "Now whatcha gonna do Ma" I was madder than a wet hen, that was a perfectly good spoon. I did what any self-respecting mother would do...I phoned his father!

Although I worked full time, I made sure my boys never suffered for it. I took them to Sunday school and they sang in the church choir. They may not have liked singing in the choir, but, to this day my sons can get up in front of anyone and speak. I once read that the fear of speaking in public was one of the top fears people have. I attribute their poise and willingness to get up and talk in front of others to those early years singing in the choir.

I was their den mother for Cub Scouts...the first day a little boy looked at me and announced "I don't think I can be in this Den, or talk to you, my mother says you're a divorcee!" I just smiled and said "it's okay, go home and tell your Mom I remarried."

Both of my sons loved art and I enrolled them in classes at the Art Institute on Saturday mornings. We got a good price, as they also helped the teacher in the classroom too.

I wish back then I would have really actively pursued a relationship with God. We went through some pretty tough situations, and for a while it was touch and go as to how they would turn out. By the Grace of God they survived their teens and twenties and I can tell you I have just about seen it all.

Michael was always a really nice kid. He caddied at the Country Club, and because he was tall and strong he double carried and made a lot of money. I always took half of what they earned. I let them spend their half on Jordan shoes or whatever it was they wanted at the moment and I banked the other half for their future. I never took more than half, because I knew they wouldn't want to work if I took all their salary. My husband and I made them work! But, more about that later.

One of my proudest memories of Michael was at my wedding. Get ready to shake your head from side to side. I have been married three times. I have great respect for the men I married, and I will not go into the whys and reasons that the marriages didn't work. I will take 50% of the blame and leave it at that.

I learned much from these men. From Rudy's father...I learned patience, and a love for Christmas as seen through a child's eyes. Michael's father gave me the strong sense of family and the structure of family that my young son and I desperately needed. Gene, well to describe Gene and I, think a nine year old and an 11 year old, we just don't want to grow up. He made me fall in love with him, after he continuously kept shooting rubber bands at me from across the aisle from his table at a convention. Sometimes he's the father, and sometimes I'm the mother. We take turns being the adult in our home.

I got side tracked there. So, let's get back to that proud Michael moment.

Gene and I would often meet up in different cities for a few days together. He was based in Seattle and me in Chicago, so we would meet whenever and wherever possible.

Our children didn't meet each other until the wedding rehearsal dinner, the night before the wedding. Many friends had flown in for the wedding so we had quite a few people for the pre-wedding dinner. Champagne was flowing, and everyone there was toasting to Gene and I, lots of good wishes and happiness.

Michael stood up and he proposed a toast, and it went like this. "Enough toasting to Mom and Gene, I want to be the first to welcome our two new brothers to our family!" I just loved him for that, and it wasn't just a nice gesture...he meant it. I was proud of him.

One of our friends used to drive me to the airport. He had two young children, and had lost his wife, and it was not easy for him and the kids.

I was flying to Boston to meet Gene, and our friend's little girl went along for the ride. "Jan, are you married?" I replied no. "Do you want to get married"

I suddenly realized where this was going and I said "Yes, I do, and I am, you see I have someone very special that I am going to marry" She was very quiet, and then she piped up with "Well do you need a flower girl?" Without a seconds hesitation I said absolutely and gave her the job. From the moment I saw how excited she was,

I started planning the wedding around her. She came with shopping for dresses, and we found a beautiful one for her. Gene and I got a hotel room for her and her father, and I decided horse drawn carriages would be great, so she had one just for herself. At the wedding I let her cut the cake, and she threw my bouquet. She was the only child there, and so she just was kind of standing around when all the music started. Michael was watching her from the sidelines, and the DJ put on "Dancing Queen" by Abba. Michael made a beeline for her, and picked her up in his strong arms, and he danced with her. Everyone else stopped dancing to watch. Her little face was beaming, as Michael held her in his arms and twirled her around. Her feet never touched the floor, and he made his entire focus on this child. All of us stood around them in a circle, and one of my friends looked at me and he said "Jan, you've just been upstaged at your own wedding by a little girl!" Al was right, and I was loving every moment of it. I am so glad another friend captured the moment on video. That was my Michael. He wanted that little girl to feel special, and he in the process gave me a memory that I replay in my mind often. Every so often the song will come on, and I can see her in her billowing white dress, smiling and him giving it everything he got.

Michael has always been the strong one, and I worried about him the most. Rudy could bend like a reed in the wind and weather a storm, but Michael was like the solid oak tree, and I never wanted to see him break. I know how much he wants a wife and children, and I pray that God will let that happen for him.

Michael a formidable opponent at a young age

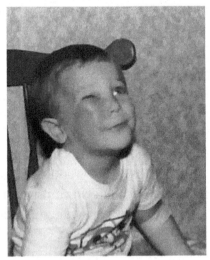

Michael with bug bite

Chapter 5:

Chuck

R udy had a really good friend. His name was Chuck.
Chuck was a quiet kid, just happy to come over and
hang with the family. You really couldn't complain about
him, you hardly knew he was there. If you needed a hand
with something he pitched right in, and whatever I cooked
he ate, and always said thank you.

Chuck and Rudy were inseparable. I asked why I
hadn't met his parents, and Rudy explained that Chuck
lived with his grandmother. As with boys that age, they
were car crazy! They took a road trip to Warsaw, Indiana
to a place called the Classic Car Centre. They went out
of their minds when they saw all the muscle cars. Rudy
fell in love with a 1970 Plymouth AAR Cuda. He had
never seen a car like this before, blue with blue interior.
They took several pictures that day, and that was all they
COULD do, as they were 18, and had no money to speak
of. But they could dream.

One day Rudy told me Chuck's grandmother died. I
asked my husband if we could take the boy in. "Jan, you

can't just take other peoples kids! Do you want to get sued when they get hurt?!" I understood where he was coming from, as we both had worked hard for everything we had. I let it go.

Chuck had a job at an automotive shop, and he was finally able to get a little apartment. The rent wasn't bad, and he had a roommate to share expenses. You know something is up, when one of your kids asks you to sit down and talk. I could see the excitement on Rudy and Chuck's face, and hoped that whatever they had to say wasn't going to be too bad. "Mom, our friend just got a jeep and we are going to take a trip to Florida!" Chuck was the one speaking, as Rudy kind of hung back, testing the waters. "We are going to go to Disney World!" "Now wait a minute! You both are pretty young, and that is a long trip. I'm against it!" Chuck wasn't giving up easy. "Mom, I want to see the ocean, and I have never been anywhere. Please let Rudy go." "No, this doesn't feel right to me. I can't stop you Chuck, and I'm asking you not to go, and Rudy YOU ARE NOT GOING." Rudy didn't give me much of an argument, as he knew his Dad would back me up.

Chuck and his friend went on the trip alone. I didn't think much about it until we got the phone call. "MAMA, CHUCK IS DEAD, THEY ARE BOTH DEAD!"

Rudy had answered the phone, and I just remember myself screaming. The boys were driving behind a semi, and an elderly lady, driving 80 miles an hour, the wrong way, on the expressway hit them. The semi saw her coming and swerved out of the way. I later heard the driver sat on the side of the road crying when he realized the boys took the full impact of the crash. I was told some Christians stopped and prayed over the boys as they were dying.

The boys had made it to Florida, and there were pictures of Chuck, arms outstretched, falling backwards into the ocean. Jason, sunburned, flexing his muscles, Chuck riding the miniature cars at Disney World. They were almost home. If they had stopped at a gas station the accident probably wouldn't have happened.

Everyone turned out for the funerals, and as heartbreaking as it was for us, it was worse for Rudy. He had a hard time and couldn't get past the loss of his friend. He spiraled downward, and went through some very dark times for several years.

In 2004 Rudy was at a pub, when a friend asked him if he was still looking for a "Cuda?" Rudy had wanted one for a long time, and he could finally afford one. He thought he wanted a yellow one, and that yellow with black contrast was sharp. His friend said, that he knew of a shop that had one, and that it was only a few hours away. Rudy took the guys number, but didn't think anything of it. He called him the next day, and was surprised that the car was original, and exactly what he wanted, but the guy already had a buyer for it. It turned out the car was blue, but since he hadn't seen an AAR in so long, he went to see it. He didn't care for the blue with blue interior, but it reminded him of that car he saw with Chuck when he was 15. He told the guy to call him if the car ever came up for sale again. Two months later, he got the call, and he bought the car. Rudy was kind of in shock, that he finally had a Barracuda, and he took his time checking the car over, once he had it home. The car was not too bad, and he noticed the AAR decals were peeling off at the top of each corner. That was one small thing to fix, and there was a lot more work to be done. He pulled out his old photos that he and Chuck had taken, in 1988. He absolutely "freaked out" when he saw the pictures, the decal was torn at the corners, and the tires were the same. IT WAS THE SAME CAR HE AND CHUCK HAD LOOKED AT IN WARSAW INDIANA! Rudy traced the car, and it had never moved farther than twenty-five miles from that spot. Fate? No, I would call that a miracle.

Rudy took years to have it restored, and his friend Ken Mosier, from the Finer Details in Danville Indiana was the man for the job. Ken had to undo a lot of mistakes that the previous shop that had the car did. He turned that car into a thing of beauty. In 2012, it took First in Class, and Best of Show, at the Indy Monster Mopar Event. It then went to the MCACN show in Chicago, where it was judged in the Concourse Gold Class. The car scored 997 points out of a possible 1000. It has since gone on to win just about every major award out there. Luck? Fate? No, I would say a miracle, and if I could see Chucks face in heaven, I know he'd be smiling and nodding his head yes.

The restored Cuda Chuck and Rudy first laid eyes on

Chapter 6:

My Girl

About three months after Chuck died I was presented with another open door. I went through that door and it changed my life.

I was the type of Mom that was happy my sons brought all their friends around. I loved kids, the side benefit being, if everyone is at your house, you know where your children are.

One of these teens was just a slip of a girl, with gigantic hair. Strawberry blond curls cascading, like a waterfall of hair. She was almost obscured by that hair.

Her skin seemed almost translucent, like she powdered it white, like those wigs the English Magistrates wore. She was quiet and respectful and after she left I asked Rudy who that girl was. "Which girl Mom?" The one that looks like a half drown kitten, with tons of hair. "Oh that's Tiffany Mom."

"Well she sure looks exhausted!" "You would too Mom, if you had as hard of a life as she has" he said. That piqued my interest and I started to dig.

"There is no electricity where she lives, and hardly any food, and her Mom left, so she lives with her father." I kind of scoffed at that, as I thought, surely my son is exaggerating the story. He wasn't. Tiffany had a hard life, harder than most of you can ever imagine. The only plus in her life was that she never had the bad experiences like I had with Uncle Wilbur. I started feeding her. I found out the kids were pooling their money to buy her products that young girls need, and I took that responsibility over. I remember her asking if she could have a new bottle of shampoo. "You need one already? That should have lasted you a long time."

I used it to try to clean the place where we stay, to wash the floor and clean the bathroom," was her answer. I was working full time, of course, and still traveling on business and was gone for several days. When I saw her again, she was almost fainting, she hadn't eaten much at all that weekend. There was no food.

I never let that happen again.

One day she showed up at my door and asked if she could use the phone. I said sure, and asked what was up. "We are being evicted, and my Dad is going to live in his car, and he said I should quit school and get a job. I want to try to call some friends to see if I can find a place to stay." I asked her a question that just suddenly appeared in my mind. "What do you want out of life Tiffany?" "Why, I would like to be the first person in my family to graduate from High School" was her answer. I was blown away, but I have always been able to think on my feet. "Oh, that's nice, would you mind walking the dogs for me for a second before you make those phone calls?" As soon as she went out the door, I told my husband I wanted to help this child. "You can't just take other people's kids, Janice..." I stopped him before he finished the sentence. "I know, you said this before, and we have four bedrooms and three bathrooms and I feed stray cats, and I want to help this girl." He then said the magic words..."Okay, just for a few nights till she finds a place to stay."

That was all I needed to hear, the wheels were turning, and I was that salesman with the foot in the door, getting ready to close that big deal.

When she came in, I told her she could stay here. I put her in the guest bedroom and as I was tucking her in that night, she started to cry a bit. "You're afraid, aren't you?" She nodded yes. "Don't worry, I'm going to take care of you and you don't have to worry anymore."

I started small, new sheets, a pretty comforter. Rudy was kind of excited about having this cute girl under our roof. She was about 16 and he was getting ready to turn 17. I had a talk with them both. "Neither of you realize this now, but you are both going to have the most wonderful bond. You will become brother and sister, but you will both be more than brother and sister, because you brought Tiffany here to us Rudy, and you were so glad that we were going to help her.

People will come and go, but this bond will remain, because you helped change her life."

Now for a moment of reflection. It all comes down to God. Tiffany told me just a few years ago that God must have been steering her in this direction. She had a very devote grandmother who prayed hard for her. She feels her Grandmother's prayers were answered. I know God put that door there that day, and I could have slammed it shut, but am so glad I went through it. Rudy once remarked, "Can you imagine just how boring our lives would have been if we never had Tiffany, I mean, look how much she has given to our family Mom." I know this; I can never thank Jesus enough.

Before I go any further, I think a little self-confession is good for the soul and to clear the air. I was a HARD mother, and I am still. Ask my family, they will verify this. I am also a hard Grandmother. Do not think of me wearing an apron, and turning a blind eye to the doings and goings on of my grandchildren. I don't.

Tiffany loves to remind me about a time early on in our relationship. She sat down to have a few words with me. I had just got in from work, and sat down to eat.

She opened her mouth, I held up my hand, palm outward towards her face. "Not now, I'm eating" I like to think it had been a tough day at the salt mines, that it was one of my 48 hour work weeks and I had a lot on my mind. But I really don't know what it was, other than that I like my quiet time.

As a little child, Rudy once yelled at me, "I hate you!" My reply, "Good, I'm glad, I never liked you anyway." He then issued a threat, "Oh yeah, well I want to go live with my father!" No sooner than the words came out of his mouth, BOOM! He was sitting on that front porch with his little suitcase. He sat there until my husband came home, questioning why he was out there. "Mom's mad, I said I wanted to live with my father, and she told me to walk there and put me on the porch. So I waited for you to come home from work, can I come back inside now?" Early on in his teens Michael and I were arguing about something, and he was angry and said "You don't even appreciate the kid I am, I don't do drugs, I get good grades and you don't even appreciate me!" my reply "Oh let me call the newspapers, and stop the headlines, Michael is getting good grades, LISTEN UP SON you are doing what you're supposed to be doing, and I am not shooting heroin in my arm, or hooking on State Street" That's your job, and me being your mother is mine! I just kind of shake my head when I think of stuff I said to them back in those days.

BUT...I loved hard too! I immersed myself in their lives (still do, asked or not) I played with them, not just board games, but crawled around in the dirt in the woods, playing army. Holidays were always something to be remembered, and friends have told me, that celebrating Christmas with me is something that leaves you feeling full of the Christmas spirit, (he didn't mean alcohol either.) I fought battles for them, (if they were wronged) and went to court several times on their behalf. Not because of any wrongdoing on their part either.

One day Michael was riding his bike, and a Scoutmaster's son took his BB gun and drew down on and pumped some BB's into the back of my sons head as he pedaled by. I was at work when it happened, I think Michael was about nine, and the Scoutmaster's kid was fifteen or so. My husband was at the hospital with my son, and watched them stick several needles in Michaels head (to numb it) while the blood poured down his neck, as they dug the BB's out. We both flew in the car to the house where the teen lived, and Thank God the police got there first, as they had to restrain my son's father as he went for that kid and his father.

We ended up in court, and the teen said he was shooting at a bird. It was an accident. I marched over to the father and his attorney and the kid (why no one attempted to restrain me, I will never know) and told the three of them, "Here is the deal, your kid admits to what he did, and he takes whatever punishment the court orders, (the attorney tries to butt in) and your counselor is going to make his money either way, but there is a lot on the line. Your kid was NOT shooting at a bird, and this is a turning point in your and his life. If you don't take the deal, I will go after you and sue you, and go after whoever gave the gun to the kid. So you better think fast." The lawyer asked me what guarantee was I giving his client that I wouldn't sue at a later date, and I replied "My word!" The boy told the truth, and took his punishment, a ton of community service. The lawyer and I became friendly and he handled Tiffany's adoption later for me at no cost. He said he couldn't charge me; he liked how I was helping this girl.

With my family, I AM ALL IN, I am always all in. They know this, and I drive them nuts, and we all know how deep we love each other. When the going gets tough, pray first, ask God for help. Then circle the wagons around whoever is in trouble. If one of us is not right, then none of us are. That's the way it is.

Those moments that I mentioned before, the things that my children have said or done that are so precious to me. My Tiffany has given me an abundance of them. I never wanted a girl child, I loved raising boys. One of the first indications that things were different became very apparent to me the day I walked in from work and she met me at the door. "How was your day Mom? Five simple words and they had such an impact on me. I was used to coming through the door and hearing "What did you get at the store" or "Mom can I — —-you can fill in the blanks here with a request." "Mom I'm gonna kill Rudy" "Michael Shut up" "I'm hungry!" and here I was walking in the door and somebody cared about my day. Awesome. It didn't take long before Tiffany became that sister to the boys. Michael was a bit miffed, at first, he wasn't sure what the deal was, and no one consulted him for an opinion. He soon got on board, he had a strong sense of who he was and he was a kind kid, as I said before, he respected women. Rudy found out the hard way that his sister had arrived. Tiffany was crabby and he was having none of it, and he called her the term that is usually used to refer to a female dog.

I heard him yell, and some shouting and he was bent over the toilet, blood pouring from his nose. Tiffany had punched him square in the nose. I grabbed her wrists and pushed her against the wall and said "that's not how we do things here." Then I turned to Rudy and enlightened him. "Son, you've learned a valuable lesson here today. Never refer to your sister by that word again." She cried quite a bit, she never wanted to hurt Rudy she was just used to reacting.

The boys were 6'4" and here is this slip of a girl trying to find her place in this family. The boys stayed out late, she wanted to stay out late. "Mom I'm one year younger than Rudy, and three years older than Michael." "Yes Tiffany, but they are black belts in karate, they are big and they can take care of themselves."

"I can fight too Mom, I can take care of myself" What she was saying was true. Tiffany was Hispanic but she was a white Hispanic girl. When she was living in the Heights she had to fight just about every day. The other Mexican girls wanted to fight her. I knew that she was tough; most kids couldn't have made it through her prior life. She was a survivor, but she now was our little girl. "No you cannot stay out late." "Fine, I will take karate too!" And she did. Not only did she take Karate, but she went to the Nationals and took third place. Our sons won lots of trophies but they never won at the Nationals. I relaxed the restrictions I had on her, but I still worried.

Recently she gave me a card. I save certain things, cards or letters that are dear to me like a broken Christmas ornament that my father had given me, my Blaze t-shirt. I always tell them "this is going in the casket with me; I want to take this with" That just cracks them up, we make a lot of jokes about what I am taking with me when I go. The only one that can't joke about it is Rudy. He hates when I talk about dying. "Will you just quit that, stop talking like that, what's wrong with you?" That is how he reacts when I give them my "if my plane goes down speech." But I'm wandering again. Back to my card. Through the years Tiffany has given me cards, I can recite the words she's written by heart. "Mama, thank you for saving my life" "I love you" and most recently "This part is going to sound corny Mama, but you know that song Home, by Phillip Phillips. Listen to that song, listen to the words.

Home by Phillip Phillips

"Just know you're not alone, cause I'm gonna make this place your home."

My heart is so full as I write these words; I don't think anyone can imagine the demons that fill a homeless child with fear. An innocent that is just happy to be, and is worried about if and when they will eat again. All these feelings are rolling over me, the love I feel for my daughter, the sadness she had to endure, the mistakes I have made, and that this guarded child that had been through so much, could feel so deeply about me. Read the words to that song again, and realize that those words are words that our Lord is saying to us. He is asking us to hold on to him as we go through life. Jesus is telling us he has a place for us…he wants to make that place our home. Talk to him.

Tiffany has done a lot with her life. She traveled to Europe and she excelled at her job as inventory manager for four stores. She married a great guy, and inherited two children in the process. Sam is in college now, a beautiful, poised young lady (who was terrified of me when she was little) and Tiffany looks at her not only as a daughter, but a friend. We are very proud of our Sam and I look forward to her wedding someday. John is in high school. Picture a good looking cowboy, and he and I have locked horns on many occasions, but we are quick to forgive each other and he has a great work ethic. He will never be without a job, he's likable, and he has no fear of work. I love them both with all my heart.

Tiffany gave me, my Lily. It kind of horrifies my daughter that Lily is so much like me, (it horrifies me too, yet thrills me.) I am so proud of all she has accomplished at such an early age and she has given back to others with her talent. Entertaining and teaching at a dance camp for children that would not have the opportunity to take lessons, and learn the dances of their heritage. One of my favorite Lily stories…I was driving home with her from a late dance lesson. It was dark out, and I made a wrong turn. Lily was seven years old at the time. I turned into a crowded parking lot that was not well lit, and cars were parked haphazardly. I couldn't wait to find my way out, and ended up in another maze and just as I turned on to the street Lily yelled at me. "Turn around, Munner, go back. We have to go back!" "What??? Why, there is no way I am turning around in this traffic and going back in that mess." She started yelling at me, "there is a child, a little child, and it's all alone and we have to help." "Lily, are you sure, it was so dark there how could you see this." "Yes, I am sure, turn around." I ducked into a gas station and turned around, fighting my way through the traffic (I hate driving at night) and turned into the lot. We drove up and down and nothing. "I think you imagined this Lily" "No I didn't, park the car, and let's get out and look" I heeded the instructions given me by this seven year old child, and found a parking space and we started walking from car to car. I suddenly saw this little girl, a toddler, leaning out of a back seat window, all alone in the dark. My heart started beating fast! "There she is Munner!" We hurried to the car, I was afraid the child would tumble out, and was amazed that someone could leave her there alone in a dark parking lot. Just as we got to the window, a startled woman sat up. The mother had been lying down in the back seat, and was holding the back of the child's shirt. There was no way we could have seen her. I explained what our purpose was and she thanked us. I took Lily for ice cream and I told her I was proud of her. There is a saying "You're never too old to learn, and never too young to teach." Lily teaches me every day.

One day while we were on island, we were floating in the water at a secluded beach. She turned to me "Munner, when I get home, I am going to be baptized, and I am excited. But Munner, I want to be baptized in God's Waters. Will you baptize me here?" There it is, that feeling again, when your heart is so full of joy that it overflows. I baptized her, and she was baptized again, back in the States. Lily loves the Lord. She wants her Papa Gene to accept Jesus as his savior and she leaves him little messages on his phone. "Papa you need to pray."

"Out of the mouths of babes comes much wisdom,"

Another miracle I witnessed was actually Tiffany's miracle. As you know, Tiffany and Jeff now had three children. I once heard on the news that the estimate cost of raising a child was $300,000. I couldn't tell you if that's accurate or not. I know college costs are soaring, and it blows me away at just how much school supplies cost. If those figures were correct they were close to the one million mark.

Tiffany wanted another baby. Me too, I wanted Tiffany to have another baby. Jeff was not on board. My son in law is one of the hardest working guys I know. His employers really like him. He does whatever they ask, and he does it cheerfully. Now who is cheerful getting up at 3:30 in the morning to go to work?

I guess, I would be, since I rarely sleep. But Jeff was a rare find for any employer. He has helped me with projects in the past, and his work is neat, he cleans up after himself, and he moves like wild fire. No sleepwalking through the job for Jeff. We all are getting older, and I understood his reluctance to take on more responsibility. Especially since they turned down my offer to purchase

Lily, (what is wrong with these people?) Now back to being serious again.

Jeff was not on board with the idea, but we went over his head. Tiffany and I and whomever else she enlisted (I'm thinking of a dear friend Brenda) were praying hard. We asked our Lord to intervene. Please, just one more baby. Sam was almost eleven years older than Lily and John was about seven years older. We wanted a sister or brother for Lily that would be close to her age. Tiffany, already praying, added her request for a girl. Me, I'd take anything we could get. Thank you Lord. Months of prayer went on and one day Jeff says to Tiffany. "You know, my truck is almost paid for, do you still want a baby?" When she called me with the joyous news that "it was a go" I remembered to Thank God, I was yelling Thank you Jesus. The day London arrived was not the day we had in mind.

Lily had the role of a starfish princess in the Indiana Ballet production of Peter Pan. Tiffany had to do her hair, and makeup. I CANNOT DO HAIR...I think that was why I ironed mine straight in the 60's and I don't mean with a flat iron. I mean with an iron! Uncle Rudy was a stage hand (he was so in love with Lily she could get him to sign up for anything) I was going to be in the audience. Then Tiffany went into labor. I raced to Harvey Illinois to be there for the birth, and was miffed that the doctor still wouldn't let me in, only one person for the C section. Tiffany wanted me there, but the doctor was adamant. I actually memorized the code to get through those doors, but thought of how bad it would look when they had me arrested. London was born and she was FABULOUS, PERFECT AND BEAUTIFUL!!! Now the race was on

56

to get to Hobart Indiana to see Lily preform. Mama was supposed to be there, and Munner was a poor substitute but you take what you get. Any port in a storm. Thank God we had a friend that was a stylist, and she loved Lily! She filled in for Tiffany getting Lily all gussied up and the show went on perfectly. I thought it might be a little traumatic for her, that her Mama missed the performance. We waited for her to come out down a long hallway, anxious parents lining the walls waiting for their little stars. She walked out, and I think she assumed that whole crowd was for her, she played to them. Dancing slowly down the hallway, pirouetting and bowing, and actually went into an arabesque too. I remembered the year before when we attended a theatrical production. During intermission, she danced in the aisles. A woman whose child was playing the lead, came over to me, and said that child is wonderful; she needs to be on stage. No kidding lady, no kidding.

This is London's moment to shine, and she is only four but she is a perfect little flower. There is no one like her Mama. We joke that on her wedding day, she will stop the ceremony "Where's Mom?" London loves Jesus and she prays over all of us, without any hesitation. Eyes, squeezed shut, "Dear Jesus, help us Lord, don't let Munner's plane fall down from the sky." Her prayers are short but intense and she has given my mother her unconditional love. GG has Alzheimer's and London could care less. She does not see old, she isn't afraid. GG is her playmate and she would spend hours on her lap, singing, napping or just being silly.

London will stop from her play, and walk over and hug you around your legs and kiss your knee, and tell you she loves you. She has been this way from the time she could walk. She is quite astute too. "Munner, why do you always have to stop and talk with people you don't know?" or "I'm a bride, I'm getting married, did you know I've been married three times?" I am positive she was mocking me.

I don't foresee her nature changing drastically, I feel she will always be this loving person, and we are blessed that she was Tiffany's miracle.

My girl with the waterfall of hair

A favorite picture of Tiffany, Lily, and London

Tiffany proving she was equal to her brothers

Chapter 7:

The Family Grows

I first met Gene's two sons on a trip to Dallas. I was nervous, Gene said, everything is fine. I have come to find out that that is his stock phrase when he is not sure how things are going. We pulled up to Gene's brother and sister in law's beautiful home, and here comes Chris, bounding out of the house, running to meet us.

He had the exuberance of a puppy, and he had a smile on his face. I call Chris the Peacemaker. If you're looking at the glass as half empty, he will do his best to fill it. I don't think he ever realized what that moment meant to me. If he had any worries or any doubts, they never showed up on his face. The boys love their Dad, and I don't care if that welcome was only for Gene, it made my evening. When Chris is smiling, it's hard to be unhappy or worried about anything. He is the youngest of Gene's two sons and the youngest of all our children in our blended family, but that does not stop him from being in the center of what's happening.

One of my Chris moments that will never leave me, as long as my memory still works, happened at Tiffany's wedding. My mother, GG as we call her, looked lovely in a grey dress. She wasn't showing any signs of dementia yet, and she just sat there smiling. I kind of hinted out loud it would be nice if someone asked her to dance. Before, I could say more, there was Chris, dancing with my mother, and he had that huge grin on his face. The photographer caught the moment perfectly and my mother loved it. It wasn't too many years after that, that the Alzheimer's kicked in. The perfect name for that disease is the long goodbye.

I will be ever grateful to Chris for that moment, him taking the time to make my mother happy. He wears his emotions on his sleeve, and I find that refreshing in this day and age, where so many people go through life, unfeeling.

Nick is Gene's older son. As boisterous as Chris is, Nick is reserved. The first time I met him, I watched him hanging back, observing the scene. Nick doesn't just dive into things, he watches and then makes a decision. Although, as a big brother, it was his job to torment his younger brother, you could tell that Nick was protective of Chris. I liked that he was his brother's keeper. Nick is organized as much as I am disorganized. When we plan a family trip, he would do all the leg work, checking to see what might be of interest to everyone. He was careful to find something that everyone would like, but cater to what each individual's taste was. And like everyone else in the family, Nick and I locked horns too. However, as a family we all work through our problems. We all took turns fighting with each other at one time or another.

Tiffany and Rudy vs. Michael, Michael and I vs. Rudy, Nick vs. Chris, or everyone tag teams and goes against Jan. I say that laughingly. Look, we are real. We aren't the Brady Bunch. But...at the end of the day we are family. My beloved cat, Pood was among the missing one day. I kept calling him and looking. I felt a tap on my shoulder, and it was Nick. "Jan, I hate to be the one to tell you, but Pood, must have died in his sleep, he's over here." I remember being so relieved and thanking him, I was so afraid the coyotes got him. Nick loves animals and my grandchildren are blessed to have such loving Aunts and Uncles. Rudy was an early on, hands on I'll hold the baby type of guy. Many times when we traveled through airports, people mistook him for Lily's father. Uncle Michael is a teaser, and he looks at them at eye level and will talk to them on their level. Tiffany is almost always available to babysit, for Rudy and Shelby, and when we went to Seattle she fell so much in love with Lorelei and Collin, Chris and Heidi's two little ones.

We had planned a cousin's trip. Collin and Lorelei just have Lily and London for cousins, and I felt that it was important for them to bond, and the Moms agreed. That trip turned out better than I ever could have planned. Lily and Collin were pretty much alike and they hit it off. London and Lorelei were two little girls happy to ignore the two older ones and just play together. The perfect description for Collin is Nice, he is a nice boy! Smart as a whip too! It's hard being the far away grandma, but our daughter in law Heidi makes sure the kids know us. I had to hold the tears back when Collin grabbed my hand and said, "Come On, Grandma Jan, let me show you my room." The things that make us smile. Little Lorelei does not take a back seat to her brother, and I loved that she was comfortable with me, coming over and climbing on my lap. Heidi and Tiffany and I just had to laugh at these four cousins. Collin and Lily had to run the show; things had to be their way. London and Lorelei totally ignoring the orders handed down by the older two. Nothing makes Lily and Collin more upset as when the younger ones won't comply with their wishes.

I watched London, who never lets her Mom out of her sight, leaving Tiffany in the dust, and following Aunt Heidi around, like one of the preschool children she teaches. The trip was a success and we want to plan more. It was really not stressful, just a group of women and the children, and it was perfect.

Back to Nick. Lily and London all love their uncles, but the minute they see Uncle Nick, its attack time. They beg him to swing them, and London insists on perching on Uncle Nicks lap when he is trying to work, and he loves every minute of it. Nick has someone very special in his life, and we all went to dinner. Lily and London didn't give the poor woman a moments rest. They climbed and hung all over her too. I think they figured, she is with Uncle Nick and so she's fair game. I don't think I could have handled it that well myself.

When Gene asked me where I wanted to go on our honeymoon, I said I didn't care, as long as the whole family went. We were a new family, all of us, and we needed to bond, not just have the ceremony and everyone go their separate ways. Gene agreed, and planned a fantastic honeymoon, a cruise through the Greek Isles and a few nights in Rome, with Egypt and Turkey thrown in. We loaded the whole family up, and by whole family, that meant not only Tiffany, Nick, Chris, Rudy, Michael, Gene and I, but Pete and Jeff too. The "kids" took over that cruise ship, Rudy took over recording the trip, and he felt Jeff wasn't doing justice to the pictures. Later we noticed tons of beautiful women from all different countries on the camera, so I think Rudy had a different idea of what we meant by recording the sights.

Gene and I loved holding back and watching them all take over that ship. We would sneak into the ships lounge late at night to observe them, dancing, or Jeff and Michael singing a duet to Santana. They loved playing tricks on each other too. Lord help the first one of them that fell asleep, or took a nap. Various props would be placed around the sleeper, and then photographs were taken, the video cam would be brought out. Michael fell victim to that prank. One day while we were in port, and Chris was asleep, the rest of the boys came in from a night on the town, at around two or three a.m. They were dressed nice, and they immediately woke Chris up. "What are you sleeping for? Dad and Jan are waiting for all of us; we are going to dinner in a half hour!!!" Chris jumps up and hits the shower, and when he came out they had all went to bed. I think they pulled that trick twice. Did Chris get mad? No, he was a good sport, and laughed right along with everyone else.

We have taken many family trips together, and each one carries great memories. Jeff and I singing karaoke, the Captain and Tennille's "Love will keep us together." The best cup of coffee ever while staying in the cloud forest. I still to this day have never tasted a peach as good as the one Jeff bought from a street vendor.

Pete, always purchasing some sort of large keepsake, like a geode and carrying it through the streets, and airports. Pete, loading up the limo with all our suitcases, and finding out when we arrive in Hawaii, that he left his suitcase in our driveway. Gene, always finding a beach chair in the perfect spot on the ship's deck. From that spot, he held "court" and every member of our family would stop to talk about something they did or seen that day. Michael, making sure we got our money's worth, when it came to breakfast, lunch or dinner. Myself, falling down on a mountain in Costa Rica, and getting injured, and having to river raft (think class three and four rapids) to our hut in the jungle, where the only medicine to be had, was aspirin. Riding camels in Egypt, and Tiffany getting kidnapped on a camel, and Jeff paying $40 to get her back. Rudy buying a great looking soccer shirt, and wearing it in Rome during the World Cup, and finding out it was the opposing team, when the boys ran into a bunch of Italian guys..."Shirt No Good" and it came close to getting ugly, but our sons, and I mean Pete too, are no push overs and the group backed off. The boys all were finding the best street food in Rome. A restaurant owner, running up to us on the street, in Athens, asking us to eat at his place on the hill, promising that if the food wasn't any good, we ate for free. The view of the Parthenon was breathtaking.

We had two of the finest meals we ever had in our lives at that place. Making new friends at a restaurant in Croatia, and trying Grappa (Grappa No Good) but dining like royalty, and afterwards given a private tour of the city by the owner. And of course, Tiffany and Jeff's honeymoon! They came on ours, so we all went on theirs. We stayed in a beautiful home, with a horizon pool overlooking the city, from our hilltop. Tiffany and Jeff had a beautiful room, with a balcony that had a gate. If you opened the gate, you could dive right into the pool from the balcony. "Mom, Gene!!!! Chris and Nick keep running through our room! They are using our balcony to jump into the pool!!!" "So?" "Mom, we are on our HONEYMOON!!" I think Rudy and Michael joined in the game too, nothing they liked better than getting Tiffany's goat.

We all played hard, and we fought hard too. When things would get too out of hand, Gene would step in. He would sit down with the persons that were having problems, and if things got too bad, he would call a family meeting. I remember one family meeting where I was in the middle of all the drama. He wouldn't let me attend! "How can you forbid me to be there, when it's about me?" "Janice, you can remember every word to any argument you have ever been involved in! I cannot afford to have you hijack this meeting; this situation needs to be fixed now! Just give me a letter to read on your behalf." My husband has a saying, "don't take the time to cry, start solving the problem." All of our family respects him, and he rarely interferes in any problems, but when he sits in, they listen.

Family honeymoon including Pete and Jeff

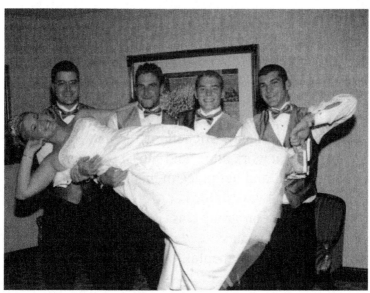

Tiffany, Rudy, Michael, Chris, and Nick

Chapter 8:

Michelle

I have a niece Michelle. We have been through a lot with each other. When I have a girl's outing planned, she is usually there. We went through some bad times too, and it was pretty awful for both of us. We both did a lot of healing and I love her very much. The simple fact is that Michelle likes to be with us. When she has things on her mind that trouble her, she heads to Tiffany's. Tiffany has a much more gentle approach about things, where I might lead of with "What! ARE YOU KIDDING ME!!!?" If anyone needs a hand, Michelle is the first to lend hers. She has a great work ethic, and she's been working hard to find herself, and her place in this world.

We would always invite her to church, and she started going with me. Our group class is small, with some great people in it. Our class leader is a man that is easy to respect, and nonjudgmental. Our church is a welcoming church, and (after the first time, where anyone would be a little nervous or uncomfortable) she found she fit right in. As busy as she is on her job, she still would make the greatest effort to come to church. Afterwards we would go out to breakfast, and then usually go our separate ways for the remainder of the day. We both would laugh about how each of us thought that the class was just for one of us. I thought me, she thought her. "Boy, I sure felt that, that was me for sure today!" "Me too, I thought it was me, its stuff that's been on my mind, and I like hearing answers to things that I need to do to change my life." We both knew we had to forgive people, and needed people to forgive us. I think my pile of needing people to forgive me was larger than hers. She was always more reserved about how she dealt with people. Me, well they all know I don't have a filter. I loved the way Tiffany put it. "Mom you are officially an old person now, you just come right out and say whatever you feel like, and think that you can just get away with that with people." Well let's face it, it was working. Seriously now, back to what's important. Michelle will be the first person to tell you that attending church has helped her work through problems and become a better person. I am so on board with that, it is true in my life too. But, like the poem says "miles to go, before I sleep" or something like that.

I was thrilled when Michelle said she wanted to be baptized. Lots of us are baptized as a baby, and years after that sprinkling of water, we end up doing a heap of sinning. The decision to be baptized was made by our parents, and we had no say so in it. We believe in making that decision ourselves. That we acknowledge we are sinners and that we accept Jesus as our Savior and the only way to be saved is through him. Do we then go on to lead more perfect lives, no but we TRY to follow God's teaching and come to think of it, and yes, our lives are more perfect, because now we are working at living our lives for HIM. We are still sinners, but we keep working on our relationship with God. "Seek and ye shall find" so we keep seeking and we find strength, and peace, and forgiveness and a whole lot of other stuff on the way. So now let's go to the day of her baptism. By the way, this just happened before the end of 2014. This miracle I am telling you about is pretty recent.

She invited family to come to the ceremony, and her mother and one of her brothers and his wife came. Michelle's brother was really happy for her. He is a Christian and he and his wife are raising their family according to God's word. There is no wishy washy faith with him. He, like us does not take snippets from the Bible and use what works for him. We believe the Bible, the whole Bible is God's word and we follow it. Make no mistake, we are not finger pointing at anyone, we know we are sinners, and we also know that we had better not judge our neighbors, because all sin is equal except the unforgivable sin of denying Christ. It's a walk that we are all on.

We were all thrilled for Michelle. We had a visiting minister, and he was preaching with gusto. Church started at eleven and Michelle was going to be baptized towards the end of the service. Her brother had a flight lesson at two O'clock and the airport was about 45 minutes away. I suddenly realized it was 1:15 and we hadn't had the ceremony yet, and he was going to have to leave. I grabbed Michelle's hand and we walked out of church to the area behind the altar and explained that her family was going to miss the baptism if we didn't get started soon. I hated doing that, but I know it was important for her to have them witness her commitment. Pastor moved things along discreetly, but she still didn't get into the water until after 1:30. Yes! We don't sprinkle, we fully immerse and it is a beautiful experience. All of us came up to the Altar to witness the event, and the church was excited, they knew Michelle and so the congregation wanted to be there too. Our family didn't leave, bless their hearts, they knew this moment was more important than any helicopter lesson. Everyone stayed to hug her and congratulate her. We knew my nephew wouldn't make it on time to the airport in time for his lesson. I called him later, and sort of apologized that things ran longer than expected. "Aunt Janice, I wasn't supposed to be on that helicopter" "Because I was late, my instructor did another walk around looking at it, and he found that there was a problem, a potentially dangerous problem! I wasn't supposed to be there on that flight lesson!!!" PRAISE GOD! I was ecstatic that this miracle had happened. Apparently the tail rotor drive shaft had a problem that could have caused a loss of the tail rotor. When you lose the tail rotor that is when you see a helicopter spinning around in circles to the ground. Something easily repaired, but potentially dangerous.

I called Pastor with the news, and a few others, and it was like a group of dominos falling over, each church member calling another to share the miracle.

Michelle was still riding high from her baptism and was relieved to know her brother was safe. You would like him if you met him. He's about 6'4" and a veteran of Desert Storm and many other campaigns, a master electrician and carpenter, and a true Christian soldier.

Michelle

Chapter 9:

I Didn't Listen

So as many times as that little voice inside me talked to me, you think I would have listened. This situation happened when I was driving home and I just wanted to get home.

I hate driving at night…I always have. I was just in town but driving home, I was in dark areas on the winding road from town. The voice inside kind of gave me a command…"Turn on your brights." I didn't do it. I argued with the voice "Why would I turn on my brights when another car can show up at any minute and then they will flash me, and be annoyed that I blinded them." Again the voice "TURN ON YOUR BRIGHTS! I actually said NO to that voice. And seconds later I hit the family of raccoons that were crossing the road. I hit the babies because they were following the Mom. I was devastated, and I cried all the way home.

Just listen to that voice inside of you, please. I tell that to everyone that is unsure of what to do in many situations. God is trying to give you answers. Just shut up and listen.

Chapter 10:

Altgeld Gardens

A ltgeld Gardens is one of those neighborhoods you don't want to get caught in. They also call it Alligator Gardens. I had a miracle take place there.

I drive, but I hate driving. You won't catch me on expressways, semis scare me. I drive in set routes, and don't like to deviate from them.

I was coming home from my mother's house on the Eastside of Chicago, and I was at the Burnham tracks. The gates were down, and there was some sort of malfunction. A train was stopped on the tracks and it was going nowhere. People were going right at the light and taking a different way home. My home was in Calumet City and I needed to cross those tracks. I figured I would play follow the leader and find the detour home. Big Mistake. I was driving and was in unfamiliar territory when my car started to have trouble. I didn't know what to do, and I turned down a street, and it was a one way street, and I was driving the wrong way. To make matters worse, there was a police officer waiting in his squad

74

at the end of the block. Great, just great. I stopped and my car was in trouble, and I was in tears and I looked at the cop, "I know, I know, I am wrong and please just write me the ticket, my car is broke and I am lost. I will be right back." I started heading towards some buildings and he grabbed my arm, and yanked me back. "Where are you going?" "I'm going up to those apartments and ask if I can use the phone. I'm lost and my car is not working." I was in tears and he asked, "Do you know where you are?" I hazarded a guess, "Dolton?"

"Lady you are in Altgeld Gardens, also known as alligator gardens. If you go up to that building you will never be seen again. People from Indiana got lost back here and they were almost killed." I was pretty naive. I had heard of Cabrini Green, but not of this place. "Is this a bad neighborhood?" The Officer pointed to a car that slowed down and looked at us, and then parked up the street. It was filled with guys, scary guys. "They are just waiting for me to write you a ticket and leave, and you don't want that." "Well let's get out of here, if it's that dangerous." Officer Larry Richardson was African American, and a tough no nonsense looking guy. He was big. "If we leave they will strip your car. Who can you get to come out and get you and tow your car?" I called the Calumet City Police Department. I had friends there and one of the off duty police came out. He was blown away that I was there. He and Officer Richardson just kept shaking their head at my lucky break. If I would have been alone, I am sure something really bad would have happened to me. I was young and not hard to look at and even if I was old and decrepit, I still would have been in trouble. I asked if I could buy the Officer lunch, he had waited so long with me. "No thank you, I am just doing my job."

I did write a letter to Superintendent Rice about Officer Richardson. I received a reply too; he was pleased to hear that one of his men went above and beyond his duty. He said that he was going to put a commendation or something in the Officers file. Remember, he could have just written a ticket and left. But he didn't.

I was in danger, and I believe that it was a miracle that I ran smack dab into a Guardian Angel, and he was wearing blue.

Chapter 11:

My Knee

I knew something wasn't right with my knee when I was walking down a flight of stairs…the pain was unbelievable, I had to sort of keep my leg straight and go down sideways, because when I tried to bend it and walk down the stairs, it hurt so bad that I could feel beads of sweat on my scalp.

I have always had a high tolerance of pain, and when this subsided I shook it off and went back to business as usual. It started to happen more frequently, and it would sometimes lock up when I was kneeling and I couldn't straighten it or get up and the pain was like rubber bands of hurt, that stopped you from trying to get up or sit down, you just froze.

The kneecap started to look worse and the whole thing swelled up and it was so ugly, my son remarked, you should cover that, it will scare people and go see a doctor. I did go see a doctor, my doctor sent me to a specialist, an ortho guy. I love MY doctor, he is our friend and treats us like family, and every doctor he referred us to was always top notch.

Well the news wasn't good. I was asked if I scrubbed floors on my hands and knees, and I replied yes. I'm old school; you can't get in the corners and get a floor really clean, unless you get down on that ground. I was also a tile person. I loved the look and the coolness on my bare feet, so I scrubbed a lot of floors.

"You have what we commonly refer to as Housemaids knee!" he said. I am seldom at a loss for words, and I came up with a joke, but he wasn't laughing. Apparently crawling around on my knees on the hard tile had ruined them. I needed surgery, a painful, long recovery surgery. He said It would take a long time to learn how to kneel again, as I would have to start with a tall pile of pillows and keep removing them, until I could actually kneel like I used to. I was not happy about the long recovery, the pain part I could handle, but I didn't want to be chained to a chair or a knee brace. We set a date for the surgery and I decided to go on vacation. I figured I wasn't going to be able to go anywhere for a long time, so I would go now and come back before the surgery.

My daughter came by, and I asked her if she would say some prayers for me, that I didn't end up in the hospital while I was out of the country. She looked me in the eye and said "Why don't you pray for a healing?" Well I explained to her that I don't pray for myself. There are children with cancer, people with major disabilities, and I wasn't going to cut in the line of prayer to ask for help with my knee. My Tiffany is not one to back down, (a chip off the old mother block) and she eyeballed me and replied "OOOOOhhhhhhh, so YOU don't think God can handle everything??? You think he is limited to what he can do!" Oh Man, she had me there. I told her I would pray for healing and asked her to continue to pray too. I left and I did pray and ask God to intervene. I tried to keep my mind off the leg, and would go splash around in the sea (I can't swim) and I would ask God if he would take care of this for me. A few weeks passed, and it was time to go home. A few days before I was to leave, it dawned on me that my knee wasn't swollen or that it didn't hurt anymore. It was pretty mind blowing, and I gingerly tested it once I realized it seemed better. You see I didn't notice the whole recovery process because like most of us, I asked God for help and I asked a few times, and then I got busy with stuff and didn't devote much time to him, and never even realized that I was better.

Once I hit the states I called up the Ortho Doc and cancelled the surgery. I then went about my daily business, taking care not to crawl around on my knees scrubbing the floor anymore. About a month or two later, something came up and I went to see my regular doctor. He immediately asked about my knee and was shocked to find out I didn't have the surgery! He just stood there shaking his head, and looking at my leg. I explained how I had handled the situation, and then asked him what I should do for the ailment I had now. He just smiled at me and said "Pray and go swimming in the sea; that seems to do the trick."

I don't push the envelope with the leg, I still like clean floors and my grandsons help me keep them that way. Every so often though I do forget and start to crawl around doing what I'm not supposed to and I get a twinge or a sharp reminder to knock it off. And I listen!

So you see its okay to ask for stuff…I don't think I would push for a winning lottery ticket, but if you are having financial troubles, ask God for a blessing, ask for a healing. He always answers, and you may not like the answer, but he does answer. I mean, if we asked God to never let us lose a loved one or let anything bad ever happen again, well we wouldn't be here on earth now would we. We'd be in heaven because God promises us joy, and there are no tears in heaven. So ask him, thank him, and praise him. When there is a crisis happening, I am there praying, praying first, always a prayer on my lips when I pass an accident or read of some misfortune. Pray.

Chapter 12:

Man at the Airport

I was flying out of Seattle at the unspeakable hour of approximately 6 a.m. I arrived at SEATAC around 4 a.m. and of course the airport was pretty empty.

I am one of those people that would rather arrive an hour early, than ten minutes late. I always have a book with me, but I also have my trusty IPAD.

My grandchildren are my pride and joy. When my daughter married her husband, he had two wonderful children, great kids. One now is twenty and the other seventeen. They already had their grandma (Jeff's mother) who is the most wonderful woman. I defy you to meet her and tell me you don't like her. It is impossible, she is amazing, sweet, and does not have a mean bone in her body. My daughter really lucked out when she got her for a mother-in-law...my son in law...not so much. So the kids had their favorite grandma, and I was kind of in the back ground, and to be honest, was glad to be there.

I had raised three kids, worked all my life, and was recently remarried, and had places to go and things to do.

Then my daughter got pregnant. I gave her the speech, "Now I raised all of you, and I travel quite a bit, so don't expect me to be around a lot to babysit, I am not like all those other Grandmothers out there etc. etc. etc." And then Lily was born…I became the insane grandparent; I even offered to purchase her from my daughter and her husband, but they were having none of it. My daughter continued working and I had Lily with me almost every day, and what a joy it was.

She was funny and witty and cut her teeth on my heart. She showed talent at an early age, dancing about the room. Not the bouncy dance of babies, but the beautiful gliding and twirling and bowing of a ballerina… along with much improvising. She danced to everything in her own little world, and it stopped me and others in our tracks. We loved ballet, but at the age of 7 we tried ballroom dancing and it was her calling. She is 10 now and dances competitively and has close to 300 first place ribbons and many medals. She dances International Latin Ballroom, just in case you wondered.

Any human that got within a few feet of me was subject to watching her videos. FedEx carriers, the air condition repairman, the meter readers, the butcher the baker the candlestick makers, all had a few minutes of their time hijacked to watch our videos. (Note I say our… we are a team, Lily, her mother and I).

So I am walking through the empty airport and there is this Hispanic man sitting by himself. Most women wouldn't be so bold as to plop down next to a strange man in an empty airport, but I am not most women. He looked sad, and in his mid-thirties. "Hi, want to see something interesting?" I whipped out my video and showed him Lily doing an intense Paso Double. His eyes widened and he asked to see a few more. I was happy to comply. I asked him why he was there so early and why he looked so sad. He explained his father had just died in Guadalajara, Mexico and he had wanted to make it home in time to say goodbye, but his father passed before he got there. He was going to be supportive of his Mother, who understandably was heartbroken. He had so many regrets, and he was feeling so much weight inside from them. I asked if he talked to God, and he said he had slipped away from his faith awhile back when times were tough, and that he used to pray and hadn't in a long time. I said, "You know, you may have walked away from God for a bit, but he never has left you, and he is waiting for you, and just talk to him. He loves you." He smiled at me, and said that he always thought of himself as one of God's soldiers, and then he asked if I was a Christian, and I replied yes. He looked at me, full in the face, and he smiled and said, "God always sends his people when you need them!" He thanked me, and we both acknowledged that there was a reason I was led to sit next to him at 4 a.m. and it wasn't about dance videos. We said goodbye and went to our gates. It was a very special, peaceful moment and I think of him often.

So talk to people. If you are a believer, come out of the shadows. You might be surprised at what you will find. Listen to that inner voice, or just follow God's lead. I'm a talker, but listen, really listen to what others have to say, and spread the Good News.

Chapter 13:

The Owl

I love that my kids think I am the person that can handle almost any problem. When things get tough they do call me in to intervene or help with a problem or just for general advice. They usually call me Mom. Mama if they are being affectionate or if something is too awful to comprehend. My son calling me on 9/11 and saying " Mama, they are jumping from the World Trade Center." I am called Munner by some of my grandchildren, as one of them tried to call me Grandmother when she was a toddler, and it came out Munner. It stuck. They call me Jan or Janice when they want me to pay attention (we worked together and they said I never answered to Mom on the job, so they took to calling me Jan) They use my first name when they are teasing or they think I don't know what I'm talking about. When they ask me to help "get the job done…or as the Italians say…go to the mattresses," they have referred to me as the Wolf, or as my daughter says, "it's time to unleash the Kraken!" I said Kraken, not crackpot.

So back to the story at hand. My son stopped over to visit my husband and me on a summer afternoon. Right after he left, I get a call from his cell phone. "Mom, there is an owl in trouble here that needs your help!" Rudy was just by our creek so I went over there with my husband and there it was. This big owl sitting on the side of the road, and it had a couple of gnats flying around its head. My son thought its wing was broken, and asked me to help it, and said he had to take off; he was late for something or another. I asked Gene to keep an eye on it and I ran back to the house. I grabbed a large box and some work gloves and a large beach towel. However, I was wearing shorts, and flip-flops, and had no protective eye gear, except for my glasses.

My husband suddenly became the no nonsense guy... with the encouraging words..."ARE YOU NUTS? THAT'S A RAPTOR, AND IT'S GONNA RIP YOU TO SHREDS, DON'T GO NEAR IT!" "Aren't you going to help me???" His negative reply was not something I will put in print. So I start off into the weeds and this big owl starts running on its little owl feet, kind of moving like a penguin and its beak is moving up and down like it wants to take a chunk out of me. Gene kept telling me to stop but I was committed to not letting this injured owl die. The owl wasn't having any part of my plan and he moves into the poison ivy! Seriously, poison ivy????? I'm in shorts, and I was really frustrated with God right now, and I sort of let him know it. I mean, here I am risking life and limb, so I looked upwards at the sky and yelled " COME ON GOD, THIS IS YOUR CREATURE, IM TRYING TO HELP IT, SO GIVE ME A BREAK HERE!!! OKAY!!!"

That owl just stops dead in its tracks and lies down on its back and I put the beach towel over it and put it in the box. It was easier to handle than a kitten.

I drove it over to an animal rescue place near us, and the man in charge put on these giant gloves and heavy cover-ups and he opened its wings...that wing spread was something to see! He said, nope the wing isn't broken. He sent it to some animal hospital and it had West Nile Virus, and they saved it.

I found that information out weeks later.

I don't recommend yelling at God or acting like you're annoyed with him. I think at that point after my rude behavior, it was more about the owl than taking the time to chastise me. But here is the way I interpret this. EVEN WHEN WE DON'T KNOW HOW TO TELL HIM WHAT WE NEED...HE GETS IT...HE UNDERSTANDS US...HE KNOWS OUR INTENT... HE HEARS US. So for those of you that say you don't know how to pray, I'm saying just talk to him. Talk to him like you would to anyone...show respect, say thank you and just have a conversation. I talk to him when I'm driving or just a quick few words at any given time. You can be at work, or in school, anywhere. Just talk to him... it's as simple as that.

Chapter 14:

Warts and All

This is a warts and all testimonial, and so here comes a huge ugly wart.

It touches on my life in the 60's. There is no getting around it.

I was an ugly duckling. I couldn't have bought, bribed or kidnapped a date. High school is not a pretty place, when you're not. In freshman year I met my best friend. He was a nice guy, a strict Catholic, and he knew how to do hair. He and his younger cousin became my best friends. Bobby started this whole transformation with me. "Janice, sit this way, let me style your hair in a wing like Diana Ross wears. Want to dress up as nuns for Halloween?" It didn't dawn on me that he was gay, until he told me. In fact, the whole crowd of nice guys was gay. This really backfired on me, as some girls thought I was running fast and loose with a bunch of guys and wanted to fight me. They had seen me coming out of the woods with my friends (we were frog hunting for biology.) The fight never happened because when three of them came up to start it, my friend Tim stepped forward and told them he would mop the floor with them if they touched me.

Suddenly I was a cute girl, and guys wanted to date me, but I was having none of it. These same guys didn't give me the time of day a year earlier. Besides my friends and I had graduated to the hippie scene, and were hanging out in Old Town, Bug House Square and Grant Park. It was challenging on the weekdays, racing home from school, telling my parents I would be home at ten, and that I was studying by a friend's. I would grab my bell bottoms and crazy earrings and we would hop a bus, then a train, and be in Grant Park by 6 p.m. I always made it home by ten, but my parents had no idea where I was. I disappeared on weekends completely.

I loved my friends, and we made a lot more downtown. Those gay kids were so funny and so messed up. Lots of runaways, and the legal age ones got us into the gay bars to watch the drag queen shows. We couldn't drink, and I didn't like it anyway, but drugs flowed freely. I think the only way I survived that time period was by the Grace of God, and I didn't deserve any of it.

I was too self-absorbed with my new friends/family. Life was hard for them, several of them sold themselves on the street, and the reality of their life was anything but "gay." The chicken queens would cruise the Greyhound bus station for teen boys, and when some of them needed money, they would hang out there. Remember, I had a nice warm house to go home to at night.

The only plus side to any of this, was it was very easy to stay "pure" since I was only hanging with the gay kids. My parents didn't catch on, because my best friend was always polite, and went to church, but it was the pageantry of Catholicism that drew him, the mystery of the Latin mass. He was fascinated with the movie the Sound of Music, and the faith that he did have tore him apart because of his lifestyle. I gave all that up, it was easier than I thought it would be. I walked out of a party on the Northside of Chicago. We were on the third floor of someone's "crib" and the kids were lighting plastic bags, the kind that cover your clothes from the Dry Cleaners. The bags would drip into a bucket and they were all on LSD and enthralled with watching the plastic drip down and sizzle in the water. Self-preservation kicked in (I thought, third floor? fire?) and I left immediately. I started having kidney problems from doing drugs. Suddenly a lightbulb went off in my mind and "I got it" that I was killing myself. I did a 360 and started dating a nice guy from high school and left the other stuff behind.

Almost every one of those kids died many years ago. The AIDS epidemic claimed the majority. Drugs claimed others. Bobby and I would have lunch and discuss his T-cell count, and he died very hard. I remember seeing him in hospice and trying to spoon feed him, and his head just lolling on his shoulders, and his mind gone. He caught HIV from an "affair" he had in California over a weekend. He had some kind of surgery on his brain, and it didn't help. I wish I would have had a relationship with God at the time. I didn't even know how to pray over him. Bobby had Faith, and believed in God, and struggled with his conflict of his lifestyle. It was a very sad ending to a person that didn't have a mean bone in his body.

I didn't have a relationship with God at the time, but he was waiting in the wings. I always felt some sort of presence, and something very strange happened to me BEFORE I knew Bobby had AIDS. We had remained friends after I cleaned up my act. He was my hairdresser, and he was living a pretty calm life too with his partner collecting antiques. I was in Baltimore on a business trip and I woke up from a strange dream. I guess you could call it a vision. I saw my father; he was dressed in white and in a beautiful place, almost like the buildings of the early Greeks and Romans. My father looked fantastic, no wrinkles, not old, very different, and yet I still knew he was my Dad. He said "Tell Bobby not to be afraid, everything is wonderful here."

I called Bobby the minute I woke up, and related the story to him. He was amazed, and he told me that today was his birthday, and he asked me a lot of questions, but I could only relate what I remembered. A short time after we had that conversation, he told me he had AIDS and that he was really scared, and had a hard time sleeping. Not a lot of people knew about the HIV virus then, it was just coming out, and I never knew if Bobby was right with Jesus when he died, but I think he was.

Ugly duckling

Defiant flower child

Headed for Old Town with one of the boys

Bobby and I in our costumes he made for Halloween

Chapter 15:

The Worst Thing I Ever Did

O kay, there are several ways to title this chapter...I could be kinder to myself and call it the worst thing I ever HAD to do, but we all know we do have a choice.

There is no nice way to sugarcoat this, it's about abortion, an abortion I had and I regret it, and it's hard to use the old "at the time it seemed right" line.

I wanted another child; I was desperate for another child. I had cancer cells frozen off my cervix, and I was due for a biopsy. I also was off the birth control pill, at the advice of my doctor. I guess the pill can escalate things. It was a scary time, I wanted another child, and now to make matters worse, the condom broke.

TMI...well that's it in a nutshell. I KNEW, JUST KNEW that I was pregnant. No doubt, but my pregnancies never showed up right away on urine tests. My husband thought it was all in my head, and to make matters worse, our Firebird was rear ended...my side of the car got the brunt, and I was whisked away in an ambulance, and before I had time to think about anything, I was getting a full set of x-rays. If my mind would have been right, I would have said there was a strong possibility that I was pregnant. But I didn't even think of it, and I was in pain. Of course it dawned on me the next day, and I scheduled the blood test to see if my fears were confirmed. They were, and I was. My doctor said I was due for a biopsy of my cervix, and he would not preform it if I was pregnant. We had a long talk and he said that I had to think about my two boys, I think they were twelve and eight at the time. He recommended abortion and asked me if I wanted to think about it, and I said no schedule it, I don't want to wait till the baby has fingers. Yes, that is a horrific thing to say, but my mind was not working right. I had wanted my husband to get a vasectomy and he was unwilling. I was losing my mind here, and trying to keep it together, and I was SO SO SO mad at my husband.

I cried and cried the night before the procedure. My mother talked to me, and she told me to stop blaming my husband, this was not his fault, and we got pregnant together. I wanted to blame him, I still had choices here, I could have thrown the dice and not got the abortion and maybe there were no cancer cells anymore. It was easier to play the blame game.

The morning of the abortion, I hoped there would be no protesters out in front; I was barely holding it together. I cried all the way there and cried in the waiting room. I was beyond shocked...I talked to other women there, one said she thought she wanted twins, and then realized she didn't. Another young girl said she hoped she wouldn't be back here in six months again. I was the only one crying. Though I wasn't "saved" yet, I believed in God and knew he would hate me for the rest of my life. Afterwards while I was in recovery, I was having a lot of pain, and it was not just mild discomfort. I was in a bad way mentally and feeling bad physically. Suddenly my body started to tingle all over, like an electric current thing, like when you hit your crazy bone, but not painful...the pain was gone and my head was filled with the words YOU ARE FORGIVEN...it was big as life, like they were written on the wall...but they were written on the wall of my mind. I saw them and I read them and I felt them, and as suddenly as that happened, they disappeared and the pain was back. When I got home that day I called my mother and told her what happened. She said "Praise God," or something very similar and said that she had been praying for me all morning and that she had asked God to forgive me, and she knew how horrible I felt. I asked her what time was she praying on her knees, because I remember she said she did that. She said about 11a.m. I had looked at the clock in the recovery area, right after I had the vision, and it was 11a.m.

God showed mercy to me that day. I didn't deserve any and he still loved me. I wish I could say I was a changed person and that I lived a good Christian life afterwards, but it wasn't so. I was still a sinner that justified whatever sins I committed. I'm saved now, and still a sinner, we all are, but I am working hard to be that person Jesus wants me to be.

Chapter 16:

The Person That Helped Me Along

I had a friend; she was my best friend...Sherry, Rose, and I were as perfect a match as the Three Musketeers were. The one that was my best friend, was not by my choice, I guess she was God's choice. She already was a born again Christian and she questioned my faith. Not judging me, but asking about the depth of my faith. She talked about God quite a bit, and I listened a little bit. But just like that mustard seed they speak of in the Bible, the seed was planted and started to take root.

I met her when she came in to the store I worked at and asked to be hired. She was kind of shy, reminded me of Laura Petrie, in the Dick Van Dyke show, and had a goofy laugh. When she laughed it would kind of come out like a sharp bark, like HAH! I listened to what she had to say, the standard small talk about filling out an application, but I was sizing her up, and before I even spoke to the powers that be, I told her "I think you will be the perfect fit here" she smiled a big smile, and shyly replied "Really" like she couldn't believe it...and I nodded. And so she was hired and the three of us became what great friendships are made of.

We all liked the same stuff…baloney sandwiches, we loved our jobs, and we loved to laugh. Our kids, in their twenties, drove us nuts. But here is the kind of friend she was. I could call her up late at night, fuming mad for a variety of reasons. My husband, my kids, and she would listen, but not with the "Oh really?" type of response, but more like outrage…"I can't believe they, (he) is treating you like this, after everything you've done for (fill in the name here, there were several to choose from) and how dare they!!!" But you see the next day it was all forgotten. I could walk in and say I had the best husband or the greatest kids, and she was thrilled…she knew I was just venting, and she never used that against me. She listened and then threw it out the window…never a "but last night, you said…." we just moved on. If I had to give her a fault, it would be that many times she looked at the glass like it was half empty…I think she had a bit of depression, but that never lingered. Life hadn't been easy for her, losing a baby at birth. She married the perfect man, a guy who was happy to stand back in the shadows, offer advice, do her bidding, adore her, and just love her with all his heart.

The three of us gals traveled to the islands and I (the one who doesn't swim) donned a life jacket and taught them to snorkel…in the roughest choppiest water, and I still remember Rose, with the sweetest accent, sputtering and trying her best not to drown and face her fears.

That trip is so strongly etched in my mind, and sometimes when I am driving at night, and that warm tropical breeze is blowing in the car window I feel such a longing for them to be with me.

Anyway, my friend loved late night conversations when she was snuggled in her bed and I was in mine and we would talk about all kinds of stuff on our minds. She stopped watching certain TV shows, she felt they compromised her walk with God...I (who hadn't even taken baby steps in that walk yet) assured her they hadn't. But you see, that's part of the seed growing. We loved going to the movies and the television highlight for us was the Academy Awards. We never missed them...seeing all the nominated movies, and then guessing who or what picture would take the Oscar. We critiqued the dresses and hair styles and spent the evening calling each other back and forth during the commercials.

And then she got sick.

She had a cough, it always lingered like a tickle in her throat and it didn't seem to go away. She had lots of tests, and nothing. However, another doctor she was directed to found what was wrong. I walked into her room just after she received the news. She was crying, and she said "I'm going to die, I have a form of lung cancer, and it's nearly always fatal." She was looking at me with such anguish, and I needed to do something... so I walked over to her phone beside the bed, held the button down, so there was no connection and said "Hello Operator, can you get me the local undertaker, I need one right away, yes the funeral director, hurry!" She stopped frozen to the spot and looked at me and yelled, "WHAT ARE YOU DOING???? WHAT THE HECK IS WRONG WITH YOU?"

I said "YOU SAID YOU'RE DYING AND I'M TRYING TO HELP HERE!" My friend, her eyes shooting flaming daggers at me yelled back "IM NOT DYING YET YOU IDIOT!!!" "Why didn't you say that in the first place," I said quietly, "and so you're not dying right now, and do you want to die, or do you want to live?" She said "I want to live, Jan, I want to live." "Okay Chickie, then that's what we will do, we will live, and we will live every day, until it's time to die."

Then I swear to you, I launched into my best Ethel Merman impersonation singing a few lines...I'M GONNA LIVE TIL I DIE...I'M GONNA LAUGH TIL I CRY...I'M GONNA TAKE THE TOWN AND TURN IT UPSIDE DOWN...and well you get the gist of it. And she laughed and laughed. You see, she loved it that I made her laugh. She laughed at every one of my crummy jokes she thought I was the funniest person alive, and so we did it all.

She didn't want to travel to Boston where I wanted to take her to see this phenomenal doctor. She wanted to be close to the family. So the three of us did everything together. We went to see Andrea Bocelli, we flew to the islands, and we stayed downtown at the Four Seasons and had massages and went to High Tea. And she lost weight, and became tinier, and still she always looked her best. She was on so many painkillers, and I almost got into a fight with some people in a restaurant, that gave her a dirty look, because she was stumbling, and sort of out of it, but she wanted to go with us to eat and we did.

Whenever the moment became too heavy I would do my best to make her laugh. One day when she was weak from her Chemo, we each were laying on one of her couches listening to Andrea...TIME TO SAY GOODBYE came on, and she looked at me, and that moment became so heavy and so emotionally charged... and I said "Chickie, do you think it is cheating, that your being unfaithful to your husband, I mean Andrea is blind, it's not like he knows what you look like without your clothes on, so is it wrong?" She smiled and we laughed and we got through that moment.

Her husband was there with her every step of the way...he cleaned the house, went to work, sat up with her all night when she couldn't sleep and massaged her aches and pains. I have only seen this type of dedication to a mother and child; I have never had the opportunity to witness it between husband and wife...until I saw them.

She wanted to go to the islands and she brought her sister on one trip and her husband on another. Her bones ached from the radiation, and the sun made her feel so much better. I watched her sitting on a piece of drift wood staring out to sea, and her sister wondered why she sat there for so long. I knew why, I knew she didn't have a lot of time left and she was just taking it all in, and she probably was having a conversation with Jesus too.

One of the hardest things was trying to get her to eat more. She just didn't have the appetite. One afternoon she sighed, "I wish I could snorkel again, but I know that's impossible, I don't have the breath and I'm so weak." I thought for a minute, grabbed a mask and snorkel and walked her carefully to a spot in about four feet of water where I knew a beautiful coral grouping was and I helped her put the mask on and I held her while she looked at the fish she loved so much, and we stayed like that for a long time. My friend looked positively radiant that she salvaged something she loved so much, from the cancer that tried to steal her joy.

The day she left the island to return home, was one of the most beautiful calmest days. And I have a picture of the water and one of her, smiling. A few days after we left a hurricane came to paradise and stayed three days, leaving everything in ruins. I was glad that she saw it at its best. We both knew it was the last trip and it was time to think about upcoming holidays and that time period is kind of a blur, but what did stand out was Academy Award time was right around the corner. We went to see all the movies, and the last movie we went to see was Million Dollar Baby. A film about a young girl, a boxer, and she fought her life and fought in the ring. She ends up on life support after being severely beaten in the ring. The movie was phenomenal and went on to win best picture. But…as the credits rolled I heard "that's what I'm afraid of Jan." I asked her to repeat what she said, her voice was so low I had trouble hearing her. "I'm afraid to end up like that; I don't want that to happen to me. I left directions, and I signed a living will but you never know if people will follow what you ask for." I smiled and kind of laughed a bit, "Why chickie, that's what your worried about??? Don't give it another thought! I promise you that I won't let that happen to you. I'll go in there with about 3 or 4 people and they will never know which one of us pulled the plug, but I'll do it.!!!" "Really, really Jan, you would do this for me, I was so worried."

She believed in me, she always trusted me, at work I was her manager, and our team was the number one team of all the stores, and she knew I didn't promise things

I wouldn't do. We were supposed to go for coffee after the movie, but she didn't feel well, she went straight home. I got the call the next morning that she was in the hospital. My son raced me over there and I prayed over her, she liked to be prayed over. Her husband was there, and when I returned back to the hospital she was on a ventilator and she was in restraints. Her husband said he wanted her to get strong enough to die at home. I whispered in her ear that this was just temporary, as she was going to go home, and I went to talk with him and her sister in that room they reserve for visiting family. Afterwards my husband Gene said he would have thrown me out of there, and how dare I get in the middle of a husband and wife.

In that little room I argued that they had to take her off, they had to let her go. I asked where the living will was. We were all crying, and her husband told me he couldn't even put his dog to sleep, let alone do this to his wife. "she's not getting any food, your beautiful wife, that never left the house without her makeup is tied to a bed, and you know her wishes, you have letters, you have the will." I was relentless. And he promised that he would have them take her off in the morning. I kissed her goodbye, and I left. I was leaving for the islands the next day, and I said I would call from there. Why was I leaving? This trip was planned before things went downhill. My husband and his son were going to the islands. Gene traveled so much, he was always in the air. I saw his son once a year if I was lucky. There was no more I could do for my friend. None of us are promised tomorrow, and it was time for me to be with my husband.

I called the hospital and the staff didn't want to talk to me, as I wasn't family. I explained I was the lady that was in there with her praying and told them to put me through to her room, that someone would be there that I could talk to. "She isn't in there, she is gone." "What do you mean, she is gone? She went back home? She rallied?" The nurse was very kind, and she wasn't allowed to divulge anything, but she said, "Listen to me carefully, she is no longer with us, do you understand, she is no longer with us." And then I knew. I knew she was with her Savior. I sat by the sea a long time, and cried, just like I am crying now as I write this. I didn't fly back for the funeral, it didn't make sense to. Whatever I could do, I did while she was alive, and I held my own memorial for the best girlfriend I ever had in my life. I held it by the sea.

Where is the miracle here, well it's pretty obvious. What were the odds that we would see that movie a couple of days before she died, and she would share her fears with me, letting me know that she needed her wishes honored? God set that in motion, he put me in that position. I haven't seen her husband or sister for a few years now. Life goes on, and our paths haven't crossed. I never wanted a best girlfriend, and she was the salesman with the foot in the door, and she sold me on that whole idea that is referred to nowadays as BFF's .I have many friendships and know great women, but none will ever take her place. She is one of the first I will look for when God calls me home.

The Three Musketeers, Sherry, Me, and Rose

Chapter 17:

The Hurricane

Yes, we did indulge our kids, but we also made sure they worked hard. It didn't matter what career you wanted. Server? Be the best server. Teacher, don't be a mediocre instructor, be the best you can be. Gene had a favorite saying "I don't ask anyone to work any harder than I do." Gene's work ethic was well known. He was successful, because he loved what he did; he continually educated himself about his vocation. He started his career young, and he kept at it tirelessly. He was on the road a lot, traveling the country working, and he rarely went to bed before 2 am and on several occasions, slept only a few hours over several days. It didn't matter if he was chopping wood, or shoveling snow, he pushed himself. Every one of our kids have helped him with certain chores, and if you are lazy, and don't have a good work ethic he will break you. He also enlisted me in several projects. Our barn had a leaky water fixture. It was May, and Gene went outside and worked on it. "Jan, I really need your help out here!" "Gene, can't you use one of the boys, I don't think I want to do any plumbing work!" (I was more the cooking and cleaning type). "Stop complaining, I dug a hole in the ground by the water pipe, the leak stems from a problem below ground, It's a small but deep hole, so I'm going to hold your ankles and lower you head first in the hole, and you..." "ARE YOU NUTS? I AM NOT GOING HEAD FIRST IN THAT HOLE. NO WAY, AND NOT ONLY THAT IT'S ALL MUD, THE WATER HAS MADE IT MUDDY, AND YOU WANT ME TO GO HEAD FIRST INTO THAT?" "Now Jan, none of the boys are around, just do it." "GENE, I AM NOT DOING THIS, IT IS MOTHER'S DAY! CALL ONE OF THE BOYS!" My son in law Jeff saved the day, it was a messy, nasty dirty job, and he helped Gene.

Another time Gene was cutting trees, and the chainsaw got stuck in the trees. He tried an ax, and did cut the tree, but it landed straight and leaned against another tree, further jamming the chain saw. "Jan, come here, this tree is stuck, I am going to put a rope on it and tie it to the tractor, and I want you to drive the tractor straight, which will pull the tree up, and I can free the chain saw. Just keep looking over your shoulder to make sure the tree doesn't fall on you." BAM! Faster than you can say TIMBER, I ran into the house, put on my pajamas, and came out with the phone. "What the heck are you doing?" "I will tell you what I'm NOT doing; I'm not driving that tractor. I called Pete, he is on his way, and in case you decide to start without him, I have the phone ready to dial 911 if the tree falls on you!"

I once watched Gene holding Chris by his ankles from the barn roof, while Chris hung Christmas lights from the roof. The chosen one wasn't spared either. I like to wrap the trees (big trees) with Christmas lights. We always start November 1st. It was a windy day, and I was worried about Pete and the boy doing the lights, but they were on it. The Chosen one was up in a tall tree, and Pete is holding that ladder with all his strength, making sure the boy was safe. They wrapped a dozen trees that day.

Every day I cook a large dinner by 1 pm. I never know who I'm feeding, but I want to make sure they eat well. When Pete is up on the tree stand deer hunting, he knows that there will be hot cocoa ready when he climbs down.

We lived a nice life, and it took a natural disaster to bring me back to earth and get my attention. It also was the first time, I completely submitted to God's will. I just followed his lead, no questions asked.

I had a lot of family in the islands, and we all loved staying there. I was heading back to the States, and the day before I left, a local islander said a storm was coming. No one worried too much about hurricanes, as they hadn't had a really bad one since the storm of 1932. This ex sailor knew the sea. I asked him if he thought it would hit here. "Yes, I think it's going to hit, and it's going to be bad, you see the sea is much too hot, the water is too warm, and it will draw the storm in." I remember looking around and saying to myself, well everything looks great, I hope it will be okay. I had his cell number just in case there was trouble. The storm, Hurricane Ivan arrived and it stayed for three days, moving 8 miles an hour, and damaging or destroying 80% of the homes. I watched the storm coming on CNN and there was this little island surrounded by all orange...that was the storm.

No hurricane hunters were reporting on the storm from that unsafe area. I was frantic. My family lived there. Aunts, Uncles, cousins, friends. Gene didn't realize I heard him, when he remarked to himself "no one can survive that" I was beside myself, I was on my knees praying for my family, begging God to spare them. Ivan was a category 5 and it was showing no signs of weakening. I grabbed my Bible and I started reading the 23rd Psalm while praying. My eyes dropped down to the 24th Psalm and I saw the words "He hath founded it upon the seas." I turned to Gene and I said I think God wants me to go there, I am going to do my best to get there and help. "Jan, you aren't going anywhere, you don't even know if there are survivors, just forget about going."

I did manage to get one phone call to my friend, at 2am. "Every tree is down in my yard and the rain is horizontal and pouring under my door." "What can I do, how can I help, what do you need" "We are going to need chainsaws, generators, whatever you can get, we will need it. The main storm will hit at 8 a.m." Then the line was dead and I couldn't reach anyone. Some reports came out from Ham radio operators, that things were really bad, massive destruction. I called the Flag carrier airline and told them I had to get there; I had to reach my family. "Sorry ma'am, no one is allowed in." I tried pulling strings. "Some of my family works for the airline, my cousin is a pilot, I have to help." "Sorry ma'am, there is four feet of water on the runway, no one is getting in." A hurricane hitting an island is way different than one hitting the US. No semis can bring help, you are on your own until a ship or plane can bring assistance. Gene didn't pay too much attention to my phone calls, as he figured I'm not going anywhere. He was kind, but firm, about me not leaving the country. "You don't get it Gene, God has a plan here, he wants me to go there, I can feel it."

The next day I received a phone call from Houston. It was head of operations for the airline, and she knew my family that worked there. "Mrs. Sanders, did you say you wanted to help? We have a lot of people from the islands living in Houston, and so many have called to donate items. Can you run a warehouse?" "ABSOLUTELY, I WILL BOOK A FLIGHT AND GET THERE ASAP!" Of course the only warehouse I was ever in was Costco, but that was a minor detail. I told Gene I was leaving for Houston to help with the hurricane relief efforts. Pete was on vacation, and Gene asked him to go with me to sort of keep an eye on me. He didn't want me to get in any trouble. I was up for that, as Pete could drive us around Houston and he would be great company. We arrived in Houston a day later, and met with the staff. "As soon as we get 30,000 pounds we are sending a flight to the island. "Great! I want to be on that flight!" "I'm sorry, but you can't, the government is not letting anyone in." I wasn't the least bit worried, as I knew God was running the show here, so I just sat in the back seat and let the Lord do the driving. I never give up control, and for the first time in my life, I gave it up to God, willingly. Don't misunderstand me, of course God controls everything, but for the first time in my life, I completely submitted myself to his will. Pete and I found a place to stay. "Excuse me, do you have a large room or suite, for two people that don't want to sleep together." That's exactly how I phrased it, and we found a perfect hotel.

First thing in the morning, we reported for duty. The main focus was generators, chainsaws, batteries and water. That was the plan. The donations started pouring in, and Pete and I worked tirelessly, and a couple of nice guys from United Airlines came over to give us a hand. Whenever we would get a boxed generator, we would open it up to make sure there was no gasoline in it (you would not believe how many people wanted to send generators filled with gas, a big no no on a plane.) I would then stuff the box with tarps, or powdered milk, and diapers and things that I knew the young and elderly would need. Each boxed generator was filled to capacity.

During a lull, I sent Pete out with my credit card to buy some generators. I wanted to help my family and friends. He came back frustrated; there wasn't a generator to be found. Apparently they had all been sent to other states that had been hit hard by another hurricane. I was standing out in the parking lot, waiting and I looked up at the sky. "Come on God, please, my family and friends need generators, please help me with this." The minute I said that prayer my cell phone rang! It was my sister in law, who lived in Dallas. She knew I was trying to find generators, and called to tell me about a store that had some left. God answered immediately! I sent Pete to the store, and he bought all 8 generators on my card. We worked till ten, and then Pete and I bought a bunch of food and boxed up 400 pounds of food for my loved ones.

The next morning I asked the supervisor for the airlines if I could fly with the cargo when the plane was full. "The answer is still no, sorry." We worked like crazy, getting closer to our goal and I added 4 chainsaws to our pile that Rudy donated. Head of Ops came by later and said the plane was taking off tomorrow, and she got clearance for me to go with the cargo, but not Pete. YES! I was so excited, and Pete got this real worried look on his face, and told me I better call Gene. I did, and he hit the ceiling! "WHAT IS WRONG WITH YOU, DO YOU REALIZE THAT PLACE IS DESTROYED! MARTIAL LAW IS IN EFFECT! YOU ARE GONNA GET ROBBED OR KILLED! I FORBID YOU TO GO!" "Now Gene, this is out of my control, and yours, you see God is running the show. I told you he wanted me to go and help, and that is what I'm going to do. I am not worried in the least. "HOW ARE YOU GOING TO GET ANYWHERE FROM THE AIRPORT, YOU DON'T HAVE A CAR, WHAT ARE YOU GOING TO DO FOR FOOD?" "Gene I got a call in to a friend, and he and another man, siphoned gas from a car, and they are going to meet me at the airport. I will take a couple of granola bars with, so don't worry, and if I need more food I will catch some fish or something." "OH YEAH, WHAT IF ALL THE FISH ARE DEAD IN THE SEA?" "You know what Gene, you are out of control and I am not going to discuss this any further, I will call you when I get back. My cell phone won't work there."

I hung up and Pete was a wreck, he did not want me going. We worked till ten, and got a phone call that Petco was sending a truck full of stuff for the animals that needed food. Would we wait? We did and Pete and I and the driver unloaded 3000 pounds of food and cages from that semi. We then went shopping for a little cooler on wheels for me, and a back pack and we went home and wrapped more boxes and worked all night. I was pretty excited and it was hard to say goodbye to Pete, but I felt invigorated. A woman spoke to me at the airport, and inquired where I was going. I asked why, and she said she was compelled to pray over me!!! She did, and I loved that! I carried some photos of my grandchildren, and the little children that they played with on the island. I thought they would be a good inspiration and I liked looking at the pictures.

I got to the check in counter, and told the young man I was on that flight. "No ma'am, you can't be on that flight, the island is destroyed, no one is going there." I told him, he needed to go check because I WAS on it, and he talked to some people, and saw I was correct. "Why are you going there?" he asked me. "Well, God is sending me to help." was my reply. "WAIT, don't go yet, tell me everything, I want to tell the members of my church about this, I want to witness to them." So I told the story from the beginning and he said he would pray for me too. As I walked across the tarmac to the plane, that voice inside of me said "Call your husband!" I said, no way am I calling him, he bit my head off, and forbid me to go, I'm not gonna call. The voice inside insisted "CALL YOUR HUSBAND RIGHT NOW!" I was almost to the plane, and I called Gene. "Jan, hang up and call your credit card company, right now! They think someone stole your card, they saw all those generators that you bought on it, and they are going to shut your card down, and you may need it." I hung up immediately and called and straightened that out!

I knew the pilot of the plane, it was good to see a familiar face, and we shed a few tears when we hugged.

Flying into the island, seeing the destruction, was a sight I never want to see again. The sea had burnt everything. My first thought was, the island wasn't green or lush anymore, it was denuded, and the color of Georgia clay. Roofs missing, blue tarps everywhere and it had the look of what a war zone must look like after a bombing.

Inside the airport, I inquired about how people had fared. "Ma'am, five of us are living in one room, but we thank the Lord for our lives." I asked a baggage handler why he came to work, since there were not many flights. "It's all I know to do ma'am." I had brought money with me, and left part of it at the airport with people that were so grateful, though it was hard for them to take it. These were proud people. They worked hard for a living, and were used to helping other islands that had been hit by hurricanes. Now it was their turn.

It was dark when I finally made it through the leaky airport to see the two men waiting outside for me. Martial law was in effect and we were not supposed to be out after 6 p.m. But our plane took off late. Our pilot wouldn't take off until every generator was loaded, and he even filled the seats on the plane with boxes and supplies. We stopped by my Aunt's House, and it broke my heart to see her come out with just a tiny beam of her flashlight to illuminate her path. She was shocked to see me, but I explained I was leaving 4 generators, and 2 chainsaws and many boxes of food. She is a woman I have always looked up to. Cooking for everyone, inviting tourists over for a meal. A small woman, but with energy to spare. She said she would have her daughter divide up the boxes of food, and share with all the neighbors, and they would all share the generators. I explained I would send more boxes in care of her son in law, one of the pilots, and she was to share those too with everyone. I kissed her and left. The police had stopped us, and we explained I was with hurricane relief efforts and they let us pass. We drove through giant sand dunes where streets used to be. Imagine, no light anywhere, but our headlights. We finally got to the place I stayed at, and the key I had wouldn't work. All the locks were sandblasted, so we worked a long time to get in. It was too dark to distribute any supplies, my friend asked if I was afraid to stay alone, and I said I was fine, God was with me, so he said he would be back at 6 a.m. You see, I had to catch that cargo plane, it was my ride back to Houston and it was leaving at a certain time, and I better not be late. The yard was a mess, and roof tiles were everywhere, but hardly any water was inside. I kept one flashlight for myself, and some water, and then I opened up my cooler. I had a couple of pints of milk in there on ice. I offered him the milk. "Seriously, you have cold milk? You would give it to me? You don't want it for yourself?" "No, I am only here tonight, and leaving tomorrow afternoon, I want you to have it!" " Janice, I'm so excited, I almost don't want to share it with my wife, but I will!" He was laughing when he said that. I had a warm can of V8 and figured the salt in it would keep me ok, along with the water. I started cleaning out the spoiled food that was in the refrigerator, and it was so hot inside. Outside was just as bad, no breeze.

The hurricane seemed to carry away the breeze along with the trees, and all it left behind was ruin, and heat. I finished working inside, and then went outside to start cleaning all the sand off the porch, about three feet of sand. The voice suddenly popped up and said "REST." I listened and I threw a black garbage bag down on the driveway and laid down among the rubble and trash. The sky was the most beautiful I ever have seen. No light anywhere on the island, just the stars, and the moon. Because there was no breeze, the insects started crawling all over me. I am pretty sure they were termites, and the no see um's were relentless. Suddenly, I got it! I talked to God, and here is what I said. "I get this, Lord, I really do. You are humbling me right now. I am lying on the ground, surrounded by broken roof tiles and trash, and you are letting me know, that you give to us, but you can take it all back in the blink of an eye." The words came back to me, when I first left the island, how I hoped everything would still be nice and look okay. Hollow words and selfish words. It wasn't until I realized I could lose my whole family that I got on my knees, and prayed. "I get it Lord, and I'm sorry." I stood up and went back to work; there was no thought of trying to sleep out there anyway. I worked until the dawn was breaking, and the voice told me to "REST" but this time I didn't, I only had a few hours left, so I kept at it. Suddenly, I was going to faint, I don't know if it was heat stroke, or what, but my knees were buckling, I grabbed onto the railing, trying to not pass out. I saw a friend across the street, and I called to her, and she came running. She went to her cistern, and lowered down a five gallon bucket into the water, and she got a sponge and started bathing me with that water, reviving me. I started to cry a bit. "Look at me, some help I am, you have been through a hurricane, and now you have to take care of me?" "Hush, Jan, we take care of each other, that is how we survive." I was starting to feel better, when my friend arrived and we started sharing all the boxes and items that I salvaged from inside. Everyone was so grateful, and we became a family that day. My friend kept telling me we have to leave. He knew I couldn't miss my plane. I finally said my goodbyes with promises of more help. We started off to the airport, but had several stops to make along the way. I took a picture of two women, that were walking to church...everything was destroyed, but they were going to church to praise God for their lives.

I witnessed another man, sitting in front of what once was a house. The house was gone, but he waved a hello at us, as if he didn't have a care in the world. That's the kind of people they were.

We stopped to see some of my family on the way back, and I left the last of my money to help someone that lost their roof. I was talking with my younger cousins, and they begged me to take them with me. "I can't do that right now, I am flying back on a cargo plane to Houston to work. We are going to fill another plane. I promise you, when I get back home, I will send for you." I understand their fears, there was so much contamination, and everyone was worried about disease. I did send for the girls when I returned home, and they stayed for a couple of months till things started to get better again.

Everyone wanted to talk. My friend had discreetly, tried to hurry me along, but now it was "You are going to miss your plane, we gotta go, let's go." I didn't realize until I felt the burning on my ankles that I was standing on a fire ant nest! What next!

Just as we were getting close to the airport, I saw my plane; it was right over my head. I was late, and it was gone. " Janice, now what are you going to do?"

"I'm not worried, God has a plan for me, so don't worry." It was going to be a long walk to the airport; everyone was there en masse trying to get flights out. Abandoned cars were everywhere. I apologized that I was leaving, "To speak frankly, you are doing us a tremendous good over there, and would not be much help here."

Those men and women worked hard to fix the island. They took it personal...everyone was on the IVAN diet. Walking, not driving, and working and sweating, cleaning up and tearing down. When I came back in December to bring a little bit of Christmas with, I was amazed at how fit everyone looked.

We hugged goodbye, and I got out of the truck and started walking to the airport. A woman came up to me, she had a clipboard in her hand..."Are you an American?" "Yes." She said, "I am with the American Consulate, what are you doing here?" "I flew in on a cargo plane from Houston, with the hurricane relief effort. I just missed my plane, and I have to get back." "Well we have one flight going out, and I can get you on it, but you will have to pay for your ticket." "I don't have any money, but I have a credit card, will that work?" "Yes." THERE IT WAS...I remembered that little voice told me to call my husband, and I argued, because I didn't want to call, but I did. If I hadn't, my credit card would have been shut off, and I wouldn't have known it. Praise God!!!! She directed me to some people at a counter.

While I was booking my ticket, I looked over and saw a little boy. "Excuse me sir, are you Alex's father?" "Yes, how do you know my son?" "He was by his grandmother's, and every day he would play with my grandchildren. Are you leaving with him?" "I am trying to get him off the island, I am worried about illness, and it's breaking my heart." I reached in my pocket and handed him a picture I was carrying. "That's my son!!!! Where did you get this?" "I took that picture of him, when he was over, and I carried pictures of the little kids to cheer me up if I felt down. Would you like it?" Of course he wanted the picture, and he thanked me profusely. MIRACLE ALERT HERE…what are the odds I would be carrying a picture of a stranger's child, and would meet them both in the airport, in the middle of all this chaos? The Lord sure works in mysterious ways.

I got on a plane, but had to fly to Miami first, and connect to Houston. I had a three hour layover. I heard of stories of people offering $100 for a bit of ice. I arrived in Miami, and I was a mess. I didn't think too much about it, until I noticed people moving away from me. I would sit down and people would get up and leave. I was dirty, and sweaty, and my legs and ankles were covered in bites that I scratched until they bled. My hair was unkempt, and people gave me a wide berth. This is where I found out God has a sense of humor. Nothing can change my mind about this; I think God sent me an angel. A very handsome, young man (looking like Antonio Banderas) came up to me. He said he was from Venezuela. "Do you mind if I sit with you? You look like you have an interesting story to tell." I almost fell out of my chair laughing, and I was thinking "Really God, really, are you kidding me?" The man, just smiled, and I did laugh out loud and said sure, sit here, and I told my story. He stayed with me for three hours and then I left for my plane. I was headed to Houston! When I got off the plane, there was Pete, right at the airport waiting for me. I can still see the joy in his eyes that I was okay. Pete has always had my back, and I know he really cares about me as a person, and a friend. I always tell him I don't know what I would do without him. We went back to where we were staying, and I was talking a mile a minute. We got food, and I showered and I still didn't shut up. I had to share the whole story with him. "Jan, you need to rest, you need to sleep, you have been through so much, slow down. Take a breather." I couldn't take a breath, I had to call Gene and share the story with him. Gene is Agnostic, and it is my fervent prayer that he and other family members will accept Jesus as their Savior. I told the whole story to him.

"Well Gene, are you a believer now, will you see the light, and have faith." "No I won't Jan, but I have a lot more faith in you." was his reply. I continue to pray daily for my husband and my family members to be saved. That day I WAS DOING GOD'S WILL. FROM THE TIME HE CALLED ME TO GET ON THE PLANE...I DID NOT SLEEP, UNTIL AFTER I RETURNED BACK TO HOUSTON AND SHARED MY STORY WITH PETE. I WAS UP AND GOING FOR ALMOST 60 HOURS! THAT WASN'T ADRENALIN...THAT KEPT ME GOING...I WAS A GRANDMOTHER! I WAS 52 YEARS OLD! THAT WAS THE STRENGTH OF THE LORD THAT CARRIED ME THROUGH!

That door God put in front of me, that I went through was the first time I ever completely gave it all up to God, and listened to him and followed. Horrible things are going to happen in life, and we need to do what we can, and we need to "let go and let God."

Island view from the beach

Chapter 18:

Alaska

I think of this as a cut to the chase miracle…in the past I have cried or begged or asked or just whipped up a short but sweet prayer…and what I find quite interesting is the "I don't have time to think prayer!" The prayer you call out, shout out, or cry out…it has the greatest sense of urgency…and I have had a few of those. I think of Alaska as one of those miracles that happened that was God answering an urgency prayer type of miracle…let me explain.

I was with my husband fishing in Alaska. My husband is a dedicated fisherman, you don't whine or complain, you fish. No room for the get up late, and go fish for an hour or two and call it a day, fishing. Gene brought me to a place called Thorne Bay in Alaska. He goes there a few times a year, and it's a guy's trip usually. This time I was allowed along.

Alaska is BIG, the woods are BIG. I liken the air to a peppermint patty, and it takes your breath away. I wanted to fit in on this trip, I wanted to make him proud of the "old girl" and so I watched and listened. Talk about pressure...I was using his sons brand new waders (don't you dare rip these waders, they are worthless if you do) I was using one of Gene's good poles (don't just try to lift it up with a big fish on it, walk backwards while you reel it, or you will snap the pole). These lures cost good money so don't lose them...AND...don't you dare let anything happen to the sacred tackle box.

We started out at about 4:30 a.m. driving to only the Lord knows where, I never saw another car. We trudged into the woods, me trying to climb over giant fallen trees the size of a California Redwood, all the while trying to not snag the waders I was wearing. We would no sooner get to a spot, when it was time to move again. I tried not to think of bears (Jan don't try to outrun them, you are as good as dead so just fight for your life). I tried not to think about the fact that I didn't even have any coffee yet, or food, which suddenly became really easy when I found myself among the dead spawned out salmon. You can't imagine the smell, of the dead fish I gingerly was trying to step around, or over, and trying not to retch. I thought I would rather face a bear than fall down upon the slippery nasty dead fish that were everywhere. Suddenly there we were at a lovely lake...not fishing or as I refer to it snagging dead and dying salmon, but actually by a beautiful body of water. It was beautiful, and so taken by the beauty was I that I actually thought "hey I can do this." Gene got me started and said he was going to walk farther down the lake, and that when I was tired of fishing where I was, to walk down about a block or so and meet him. He also left the sacred tackle box with me. With the parting words…"don't let anything happen to the tackle box, you hear?" I heard, believe me I heard.

After about 45 blissful minutes I started to walk on the edge of the lake towards where Gene was. I cradled that tackle box, like it was my first born child.

Suddenly, without any warning the ground started to give way, and it was like I was sliding on pea gravel, I slid into that water before you could count 1 2 3.

The ice cold water rushed into my waders, and I tossed the tackle box as I started to fall, and lures hit the ground, but not the water, and I was in some kind of hole, because the ground was now at shoulder level and I grabbed twigs, grass anything, I did manage a quick feeble "help" but I didn't really grasp the enormity of the situation until the twigs and grass broke away from my hold and I knew I was going under that cold water. They talk about "Hail Mary passes" in football, A last ditch effort to win…my hand grabbed again, and my hold broke away and I was going down even faster. I yelled, "Lord help me, or more like, Lord save me."

I stretched and grabbed a skinny root and it held…I had to work so hard to get to the ground that I was lying there exhausted and crying, from the fear of what had just happened to me. God heard my short, feeble prayer of urgency and he saved me, and I can't even remember if I thanked him at the moment, I was so done in, and it shames me to think I might not have thanked him.

Gene walked up a few minutes later and looked pretty shocked, and asked if I yelled help, and I said I did, but just not loudly, as I didn't realize the danger I was in. He said "JAN IF YOU ARE IN TROUBLE YOU GOTTA YELL HELP AT THE TOP OF YOUR

LUNGS!" He was shaken up too by what had almost happened, in the middle of nowhere, and here's the deal folks...God heard my prayer, my short prayer of what I needed, and he answered me immediately.

Nowadays, I thank him out loud quite a bit, and I ask forgiveness too. I also think about the fact that when you are really in trouble, when you are facing insurmountable odds, when death is at the door, you need to have his name on your lips, even if it's the last words you ever speak. Call on Jesus, there's power in that name... shout it.

Fishing in Alaska

Chapter 19:

The Stray Cat

fed stray cats. I would try to catch them, and so far I had caught two males and had them neutered. Pood and Blondie didn't hold that against me, and they liked the accommodations, so they stayed. My son in law Jeff built a house for my cats and inside the house were those plastic igloos that you can buy at any pet store. Pete set up some heat lamps inside, and it was quite cozy for the cats. Pood and Blondie were very friendly and affectionate for feral cats.

One day I saw a beautiful black cat, it looked like an angora, but I don't really know much about types except for Siamese. He had long hair and came around to eat. He didn't fight with the other cats either, just ate and left.

Well it was my wedding anniversary in a few days and Gene and I were going to San Francisco to celebrate. I had never been there, so I was looking forward to it. The airline tickets were purchased and all the plans were in place. The black cat came by and I fed him and he started purring and rubbing against my leg, so I reached down to pet him. WRONG...he immediately bit my hand, really bit it and it was bleeding and felt like needles hitting my bones. I yelled and he took off. I washed my hand and applied ointment and called my mother in law. Gene's mother was a retired surgical nurse. She was horrified! "Jan a cat bite is serious, very serious, and you need to go to the emergency room."

Mom was a no nonsense woman, and not one to panic over nothing, but she got my attention over this and I headed to the hospital. By now my hand was swollen up twice the size and they soaked it at the emergency room and started explaining that I would need rabies shots because the animal attacked for no reason. The cat had acted friendly and then suddenly bit with a vengeance. The Gamma Globin shot was about $1500 and they told me I needed to catch the cat if at all possible to avoid getting the series of shots. Oh did I mention I was supposed to leave on the trip the next day?

I was in tears when I told Gene I couldn't go on the trip because I had to monitor this bite and try to catch the cat for testing. I was in a lot of pain, and he understood and felt pretty bad for me. I called animal control and they brought a cage for me to try to catch the cat. I put a can of cat food out as bait. Gene left because he had business in San Francisco and I sat around watching and waiting and worrying. The black cat showed up several times, but avoided the trap each time. I only had a few days to get this done or I would have to start the series of shots, so I was panicking. Animal control said they were coming to get the trap in the morning (they only gave it to me for a few days) and I was beside myself. I said a prayer, nothing fancy, please God, I gotta catch this cat. I am out of time and I need your help, please! I went to shut the garage door, and lo and behold I see the cat walking down the driveway. He acted like he didn't have a care in the world, just kind of sauntering, and I was barely breathing, saying over and over, please, please, please get in the cage. I watched from the house and that cat walked right up to the cage and just walked in. Just like that! The door snapped shut, and he turned into a spitting, howling Tasmanian devil!!! I was now terrified of him. I had a hard time getting up the nerve to even pick the cage up as he was quite a spitfire! I was afraid of getting bit through the cage.

Well I took that cat to the vet, and found out they would have to kill him to test for rabies. Ohhhhh, I didn't plan on that. My vet observed him, and thought he didn't have rabies, and I took a chance and didn't have him killed. The vet watched him for so many days, and pronounced him rabies free. "Jan, what do you want to do with him, he's beautiful, and we may be able to find him a home." I was all for him having a home, any home, just not mine. So I said, "Neuter him!" They did, and he found a home. Gene thought it was pretty funny, he felt I had the surgery done as retaliation. He liked to say, "Yah Jan, something crosses you, and you go for blood, you neuter him." I told him to watch his step and remember that.

Seriously folks...that was a miracle in my book. I needed that cat caught, I was out of time, and I asked God, and he got the job done.

Chapter 20:

The Chosen One

A huge door was in front of us. God put it in front of Tiffany first. She came to me one day, and told me she was in contact with a nephew. Her brother fathered numerous children, and he left them. The kindest thing this boy's parents did for him was to abandon him. His father was already among the missing and his mother asked a kind Christian woman to watch him while she grocery shopped, and she never came back for him. This lady was already caring for a grandchild that Tiffany's brother had fathered with her daughter. The boy was no relation to her, but she fell in love with him on sight. I think he was about six months old.

It wasn't an easy life for her, caring for two little ones, but she raised them in the church and she gave them unconditional love. The boy was older, and she was ill, and she couldn't care for him, in the way you care for a headstrong teenage boy. Mrs. Foster, as I will refer to her, found Tiffany and called her, and Tiffany took the boy under her wing. I think you can imagine just how much trouble a sixteen year old boy can get into, especially one that hadn't had a lot of supervision and was used to doing what he wanted. I asked Tiffany why she wanted to take all this on her, "Mom, you saw something in me, and I see something in him, I think we can help him." "Okay, then, that's enough for me, but remember it won't be easy." I saw something in him too, though it was difficult at first, as he never spoke much and had a sullen expression on his handsome face. Things were going okay, and he was living with Tiffany, and then everything hit the fan. He got in some trouble at home, nothing too terrible, but Tiffany and Jeff were on their way to church and she was distraught and she called me.

I came by and picked him up, and I talked to him. I asked for the truth, the whole truth, and he gave it to me. He didn't sugar coat anything. He had a strong dislike for men, all the men that had been in his life had either been cruel or disappointed him. He loved his grandpa, but he wasn't well either, so he couldn't do much physically with him. I offered him a "golden ticket" just like in Willy Wonka. If you get on board, I will take you as my grandson. We will work hard to change your life. He looked at me, and nodded yes. I told him I expected a B average in school. I gave a whole list of things I expected. Our talk was over, and I dropped him off at Tiffany's, and he jumped out of the car, and then turned and came back. He put his arms around me, and his head on my shoulder and told me he loved me. That did it! I was so in, and I knew there would be no turning back. He didn't know what to do with his life, and thought his only option was the armed forces. He then told me always wanted to be a Fireman when he was little. He graduated high school with the B average, and then we got down to business. I used to have a youth group in my other church, and there was a great kid named Jake. A real likable kid, that didn't have a mean bone in his body. Jake excelled in college, and then his Grandmother got sick, and he took a year off to care for her. I asked him to be a study partner for my new grandson. Work with him, and help him pass the college entrance exams, and what I really wanted was to find males that would be a positive influence on this guarded kid. Jake was 20 when we started, and they both had a love of guitars and they bonded. I called up another friend. Mike was an ex-boxer, ex police man, and working as an Inspector for the railroad, in their homeland security division. I hadn't talked to him in thirty years, and when I called him, there was no hesitation in his voice. He was on board. Mike and his wife are Christians and they attend church every week. He taught my grandson how to box, and a lot of other things that a man needs to know. Mike was used to interviewing candidates that wanted to work for him, and he taught the boy how to act during an interview. Mike showed a genuine interest in him, and he and his wife had my grandson over quite a bit.

Another friend Justin, worked for the fire department and he took an interest too. I already enlisted Uncle Pete to teach the boy how to put in a hard day's work. Pete started out as a good friend of my son Rudy, and he became our son too. He and I both loved Japanese Maples and he helped build a gold fish pond and did a tremendous job landscaping my yard. He is a fixture at our house, either helping or hunting during deer season.

It was Pete that gave my grandson his nickname. One day I called him, and asked what he was doing, "I'm having lunch with your two boys Jan, Rudy and Michael and we think you are spending way too much time with the Chosen One, and we are figuring ways to off him." We both started laughing and the nickname stuck. The chosen One. My grandson took a lot of ribbing for that name. Writing this down, it all sounds easy, but it wasn't. I was light years removed from his generation. I don't filter my thoughts, and we went head to head and toe to toe. I thought, I am way too old for this and then I remembered Noah. Noah was over 500 years old when God called on him! I stopped complaining.

The Chosen one lives with Gene and I now, and he has graduated the Fire Academy, and Graduated EMS school, and is working towards his Fire Science Degree. He is 19, and he is doing great things with his life. He is doing great things with my life too. You see, I thought God brought me into his life to help make him a better person. And then one day, I remarked about how someone was just messing up terrible and he looks at me and says, "I don't want to judge them, Munner, I don't know what their life has been like or what they have been through, so I really can't say anything about this person." I felt about six inches tall. IT HAS DAWNED ON ME THAT GOD HAS PUT HIM IN MY LIFE TO MAKE ME A BETTER PERSON.

I received a bonus here too. Mrs. Foster has become very dear to me. We talk every day and she has helped me take great strides in my walk with God. Her faith is stead-fast…when I'm not too sure what course of direction to take, we both pray, and STAND…we stand and wait and have faith that our Lord will give us answers. She told me how hard she was praying for help for the boy. She has a lot of health issues, but she never complains and she was thrilled that God answered her prayers and brought Tiffany and I in. She is my Grandsons Mama, and I ask God to watch over her...we love her, and the boy and I both need her.

We still argue, sometimes heatedly, and recently I talked with Pete. "I can't relate to this generation Pete, and I get so frustrated." "Jan, look how far he has come, focus on that, you have high expectations and that's good, but focus on today, and it will all happen, and if he gets too difficult I will hit him upside the head!" I look at the man my grandson is becoming, strong (he is really into taking care of himself and working out), handsome, self-assured and making a life for himself. I pray over him every day, I pray for all my grandchildren. He prays too. Yesterday I asked him how he was handling certain problems and he told me he prays more and asks God for help. That's it, just recognize, and pray and ask for God's help. And go through those doors, open them... miracles await you.

Dear Mrs. Foster and her boy

The Chosen One

Chapter 21:

My Blessed Miracle

My church is Pentecostal. We follow the Bible, the whole Bible. A main focus is the Baptism of the Holy Spirit, which is evidenced by speaking in tongues. It is a language spoken between you and God. There are many references in the Bible. Acts 2:4 "And they were all filled with the Holy Ghost, and began to speak with other tongues, as the Spirit gave them utterance." 1 Corinthians 14:2 "For he that speaketh in an (unknown) tongue speaketh not unto men, but unto God: for no man understandeth (him); howbeit in the spirit he speaketh mysteries. Mark 16:17 "And these signs shall follow them that believe; in my name shall they cast out devils; they shall speak with new tongues."

This was something that troubled me. Was it real? I was new to this church, and I saw many people doing this, and I confess that I was fence sitting here. Was it for show? It was hard for my mind to accept this. I had not been avidly seeking God, but he was avidly seeking me. This skepticism was like a huge stumbling block in my walk.

I attended services one day and we had a visiting Evangelist (I think from Alaska) and he started preaching, about having anger, or hate, and that you cannot expect to see God if you hate your neighbor. My Pastor had preached this before too. I had a ton of anger, and I was trying to move past the hate. I am not writing this testimonial to air my family's wrongdoings, or expose their faults. So it is important for you to know that many horrible things have happened in our lives, but we have endured. My faith has carried me through so much. I loved my husband, but I was angry with him, (that word doesn't begin to describe the depth of anger I felt.) I was trying to let go of my hate for others that had tried to destroy my marriage. For four years, I did not like my husband, but I loved him. It was a time in my life that brought me to my knees.

I prayed, I claimed my marriage and my family in Jesus name. I had friends pray. I was still in the woods, but things were a bit better, and I was a lot better.

Forgiveness is huge. It is essential to Salvation. It is essential for good health. Did you ever lie in bed at 3 a.m. seething with anger, and replaying things in your mind, over and over? Have you ever held on to anger or hate that it consumes you? Well I have. I listened to these words the Preacher was saying, and he said that if you feel this way you need to come to the altar and leave that hate, and bury that anger. It was an altar call. I practically ran up there, in fact I was the first one up there. My church family prayed over me, they anointed my forehead with oil. Tears streamed down my face and

I forgave and asked for forgiveness. I returned back to my seat and stood next to one of our church leaders. He prayed with me. I prayed hard. I remember he asked if my heart was clean, and I said it was. I shut my eyes and I prayed to God, and my throat started to tighten, and all of a sudden it happened. The Holy Spirit came over me and I was speaking in tongues. I did not plan this; it was not for show, it just happened. I will try to describe this to you. If you hold your hands over your ears, and talk, your voice sounds different. I didn't have any control over what happened. Words just came bubbling out of my throat, and my mouth, and it was a language I did not know. It was like a waterfall that just happened and it was the most blessed gift God has ever given me. Afterwards, I asked this man if he could hear me. "HEAR YOU? THE HOLY SPIRT WAS LIKE AN EXPLOSION COMING FORTH FROM YOU" Wow, what could I say after that. An analytical friend of mine, said "Jan, it's obvious you were under mass hypnosis." I burst out laughing at that. I was there, I was present, I was at prayer, and I was not under any influence of any drug and was not hypnotized. I shared my experience with my children. Rudy asked me, if someone video-taped me? He wanted to see it. "No son, I wasn't video-taped, this wasn't a show." My darling Tiffany (who has received the gift of the Holy Spirit many times) chimed in "Of course it came out like an explosion Mom. You are such a control freak, and never want to give up that control! The Holy Spirt had to explode out of you!" We both laughed, I just love that girl.

I find I want to be in church more. I miss my church when I am gone, and I have started bringing the sermons on CDs with me. What used to be a trial, sitting through a long service, is now welcomed. God is changing me, and I find that it is getting easier to give worldly things up that seemed so important before. I know now and understand what my friend meant, when she said she didn't want to watch certain television shows anymore. I get that now.

I thank God for my church, and our Pastor and our congregation. Someone suggested I visit other churches. I said, I did, in the past, and something was missing. When I walk through the doors of First Apostolic Church, of Steger (Illinois) I am home. There is that song again by Phillip Phillips, "Home. I'm going to make this place your Home." Thank you Jesus.

As a kid I coasted through church when I was forced to attend. As an adult, I did my part and put my sons in Sunday school and choir. I enjoyed working with the teens in my youth group and it kept me out of the sanctuary, where I would have to stifle a yawn during the sermon. BUT I have finally found what it feels like to be in a church that is so filled with the Holy Spirit, that you WANT to attend, not just on Sundays, but on Thursdays too. You want to get on your feet and raise your hands and sing and shout out praises to God! You crave the teachings of the word from Bible study and you feel more alive during your worship, than you ever felt at any rock concert. And when people pray for you, they pray from the depths of their soul and lay hands on you praying for a healing of whatever is troubling. A church where you shed tears, that cleanse your heart, and wash away everything that stands in the way of your walk with God! And when you walk through the doors you feel the power and are greeted like dear family members! A church where voices are lifted in prayer, not in repetition, but in earnestness of the needs of the people. Where GOD is truly in the HOUSE! That's MY church people! Steger Apostolic.

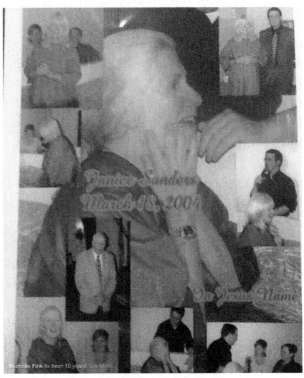

Most important day of my life

Chapter 22:

The Men I Married

One day my mother was talking to a friend and mentioned I was getting married. "Carol, you mean Janice is getting married again? This will be the third time!" "NOoooooooooo Gin, you are wrong, she hasn't been married three times...wait, I guess you are right."

I owe so much to the men that I married. I owe them apologies, and I owe gratitude. Each one has been an important part of my life. I am so grateful that they have remarried to women that truly make them happy. Two gave me my sons, one, supported me in the decision to take in my daughter. I learned how to cook, how to be patient, how to surround myself with noisy family. And one, gave me free rein to just be me, and accepted a Grandson, without ever even being asked.

The only changes I would have made in my life would have been to have a relationship with my Lord and Savior a lot sooner. I have always done my best to help others, and Gene has given me the ability to do that on a much larger scale. I do my best to live by my favorite

Bible Verse. Luke 12:48 "For unto whomsoever much is given, of him shall be much required: and to whom men have committed much, of him they will ask the more."
For Gene, the head of our family circus. I share the words of my favorite song, by the Beatles.
In My Life by The Beatles
"But of all these friends and lovers, there is no one compares with you."

Approximately one year before marrying my son Rudy's father

Same time period

Taken shortly before marrying Michael's father

Gene and I 2014

Chapter 23:

My Father's Death

My father was a good man. He prayed every night. He worked as a store clerk for the railroad. He was honest, really honest. "Hey Harry, this fell off a truck, I can give you a TV cheap." "No thank you." Dad was always there for us, and I wished I would have spent more time with him in the later years. Sure I was there for holidays, but when he would call, I would wish I could just get off the phone, I had stuff to do. He just wanted to hear my voice. I would give everything to just hear his voice again now.

He had a stroke, and he couldn't talk. He was in the hospital and we took turns siting with him. He took a turn for the worse, and I stayed. I remember sleeping in a chair with my head on his bed, and waking up and seeing him staring at me. His eyes said everything..."Why are you here, it's dark, and I'm worried about you?" He was easy to read. I looked at him, and I told him about the stroke and that I didn't want him to be alone and that I was there for him. He suffered a lot in the hospital. He was always breathing through his mouth and couldn't swallow and if you try that for a bit, you will see just how dry your mouth gets. I would swab his mouth out with some kind of cooling gel. Every so often they would come and suction out his throat. It was painful; you could see how he fought it, grabbing at the nurses and trying to stop them. I took his hands in mine. "Dad you said we were tough, you always said the first punch is half the battle, and that we should never be afraid. You are a tough German. This has to be done." He looked at me and he got it. He didn't fight the nurses anymore, he just endured.

I was the only one with him the day things changed. He was breathing peaceful and the monitor showed his numbers going down. A nurse came in and asked if I wanted a Priest. I said no, I was going to pray with him. Just leave us. I put my arms around him, and said the Our Father, and the 23rd Psalm. "Dad I know you lost your mother when you were so young. Its okay, go with her. I will take care of Mom, she will be fine. There is nothing to be worried about. I love you Dad."

The nurses had called my family and they were on the way. I watched the monitor numbers go up, and so I knew he heard me. Then they started dropping. 30, 20 and as I held him in my arms, I watched death move over his face. His color changing. What happened next was one of the most powerful things I ever experienced. He died, and at that moment, something hit me…passed through me, something wonderful. My husband arrived seconds later, and I watched my mother and family, heads bent over my father's bed crying…but it was like I was looking through a window watching them. I felt far removed though I was only a few feet away. My husband took my arm and led me out into the doorway "Janice, are you okay?" "Yes." "No, Janice, are you really okay, are you sure? You're smiling!" "I am wonderful." I said, and I could see the shocked look on his face, why wasn't I behaving like everyone else, they were overcome with grief, and here I was smiling. I can tell you that when my father's soul, his spirit left his body, something happened to me...something wondrous. Recently, I spoke about it in my class at church. A member of our church who was Jewish said that he thought I had been touched by the Angel that God sends when people die. He said the Jewish faith believes this. I don't know the answers here, but I know something happened, something that was not of this world, and it made me start thinking more about God.

My father, a good man that had a hard life

Chapter 24:

My Sister

I have told my children the two hardest lessons they will need to learn are life is not fair and to forgive those that hurt you.

The Bible says there is no way of getting around the forgiving part. God gives you the amount of forgiveness that you give others.

I have finally climbed that mountain of forgiveness. The list was long of those that have hurt me, and I have truly forgiven them all. The list is longer of those who need to forgive me.

My sister and I have always been competitive. Board games would become so heated. During a game of Risk, my husband walked over and tossed the game out the door after listening to the back and forth arguments. Scrabble was even worse.

The last few years we became estranged. I honestly can't remember how it started. Dad always said, "It takes two to tango." And we tangoed a lot. Things have gone way over the top and the whole family was hurt over this estrangement.

Lori and I are both Christians, and there is nothing a non-Christian loves more than to see two Christians behaving in an unchristian like manner. The funny part is that we have always been proud of each other. My favorite Lori story that I love to share goes back to when she was a teenager. She worked part-time in a nursing home as an aide. A fire broke out and everyone was being evacuated. The Fire Department was on the way and there were elderly people that couldn't be moved easily. She was advised to shut the fire proof doors and leave, but she didn't. She couldn't walk out on them, so she stayed until the Fire Department arrived and put out the fire.

Another Lori story was when she was a flight attendant for Cayman Airways. She was new on the job. A large male passenger became unruly and hit a woman and jumped up in the aisle. My sister got behind him and grabbed him in a bear hug. He was stomping on her feet and she was hanging on for dear life. Finally the others helped her to subdue him while the pilot landed the plane. The "aha" moment was when the police boarded the plane and the man pushed the officer's hand away. He was immediately lifted out of his seat by the lapels of his jacket and the burly cop told him, "Listen buddy, this is no stewardess you're messing with, this is NYC Police Department!!!" Lori said the man suddenly became very meek and walked off the plane with them. HOWEVER, I will put my sister's bravery up against anyone. That officer didn't know what great backup he had in Lori.

I recently saw my sister and hugged her and asked her for forgiveness and we talked about life being too short for this foolishness etc. I am so glad that she found it in her heart to forgive me. I love her with all my heart, and we have started paving the road...the first blocks of forgiveness are laid.

My mom and my sister, I love them both

Chapter 25:

Goodbyes

When I used to ride the train downtown, I would pass a cemetery and as I stared out the window at all the gravestones, I wondered what those people were like. Were they good, were they bad, did they have families that missed them. Did they have time to say goodbye? That's the thing that really stuck in my mind.

I was still in my teens, but I remember asking God a favor. "God, when it's my time to go, please give me time to say goodbye to people. I don't want to just go to sleep and not wake up, I don't want to burn to death either, but please let me say the things I need to say to people before I go." When you think of it, it was kind of nervy, I mean I rarely attended church and here I was asking for the moon.

The Illinois Central Railroad crash reaffirmed that. I thought about everyone on that train that died. Did one of the ladies that died kiss her husband goodbye?

Did any parent have a fight with their child? I didn't lose sleep over it, but I thought about it a lot. I asked God again, for that request. I didn't think of it as a prayer, I just looked at the fact that someday I was going to die, and I wanted him to know my thoughts about it. Pretty silly, when you realize he knows what you want before you even ask for it.

September 11th, 2001 really brought it home. So many of those people that knew they were going to die, phoned their loved ones. I wasn't the only person that thought that way. I believe that many of you think the same way too. The one thing I don't fear is dying. I don't want to go yet; I want more time, just like most everyone else. Sure I worry when I find I have something wrong with me. I attribute that more to the fact that I have trouble letting things go. I am not sure which alphabet disorder I have, but I think I have one of them. When I start to obsess, Tiffany starts singing that song from the Disney movie "Frozen"…I have to laugh, and I do LET IT GO for a time.

It wasn't till recently that I realized God was answering that prayer of mine. He was answering it in reverse. I started putting two and two together, and it was pretty amazing and it fills me with a sense of wellbeing that I have these moments to treasure.

Recently a dear, dear friend of mine fell and broke his hip. That is a bad thing to happen at any age, but he was 90. This man took a chance on me, and hired me. We worked together for 23 years, and he is very dear to me. He and my brother taught me all about business, and I learned about life too. We all loved what we did, and after my brother opened his own store, I stayed on to manage the store that had hired me. My buddy and I laughed about everything, and we shared stories about our families, we played cards, and we were great friends. He was retired and lived with his son and daughter in law, and had a great life there.

I was out of the country when I got the text message that he fell and broke his hip. I called and talked to his family and they told me his surgery was scheduled for tomorrow. He was sedated and I asked if they would hold the phone to his ear, so I could speak to him. "I don't think it will do any good Jan, he is pretty out of it, and he is on morphine, but we'll try." They put the phone by his ear, and I told him how sorry I was, and how much he meant to me, and that I loved him, and he was going to get through this. I said I would make him my priority and visit when I got home. His son said "I'm sorry Jan, but he isn't responding…" I could hear his wife in the back ground, "Wait, wait, he's waking up!" And I hear my friend calling my name. He spoke to me in as clear a voice as if nothing was wrong. He told me he loved me and that he missed me and he was fine and it was a moment that I will always treasure. He died a few days later, and I flew home for his funeral. I am blessed to have met this man and his wonderful family, our friendship is such a strong bond.

Remember the conversation I had with my best friend, before she died, where she shared her wishes with me? That is another example of having the time to say what is needed. I was with my father when he died. He died in my arms. I prayed over him, and I watched the monitor as I spoke to him, telling him it was okay to go, and I knew he heard me, as it rose upwards, and when I was done speaking, and praying the numbers went down and he passed away.

My brother, my dearest brother. I loved my brother with all my heart. I had him in my life for over 60 years. He was my protector and my hero. He was the type of person that would bleed out of his eyes before he asked anything for himself, but he touched so many lives with his generosity. Not just his check book, he gave of himself. I remember seeing an elderly lady at a family function and inquired who she was. It turned out her son had passed away; he was one of Ronnie's friends. My brother made it a point to invite her to everything, so she didn't sit home alone. That was the kind of guy he was.

One day we were at work, I was newly hired and a raging snow storm was going on. Business was at a standstill. I saw an elderly couple gingerly walking across the parking lot, holding on to each other. We all wondered why they were out on a day like this. They came in the store, and I went to wait on them.

"We brought a few things to show you, to see if they have any value, if they do, we sure could use the money." I looked at the items, stuff you throw in a kitchen drawer, and keep, and there was nothing there. Nothing of value. I asked them to wait, and hurried over to my brother. "Ronnie, oh my gosh, it's junk, what do I do, how do I tell them, there is no value?" He walked over there, and said "Jan, asked me to take a look at what you brought in." He poked around and examined each item. "Well folks, there isn't much value here, I'm sorry to say, it's only worth $25 dollars." Their eyes lit up and they were thrilled. My brother took $25 out of the cash register and gave it to them. After they left, he walked over to the cash register and took $25 out of his pocket and replaced it in the drawer. "Jan, when people look like they did, and you see the need; you can always find a way to help them." He then put the items in the trash can and went back to work. I never forgot that lessen that he taught me, and I try to follow in his footsteps.

My brother was disabled and he was not well at all. We wanted him to go to the hospital and he didn't want to go. He prayed every day, and he had a strong faith in God and though he was in a lot of pain, his faith never wavered. He called me one night, and I could hear the pain in his voice. I begged him to go to the hospital. "No Jan, I am not doing that, but would you get me a new wheelchair, mine broke and I really need one." "Absolutely Ronnie, whatever you need, and I will order it right now, and I will call you back." I then pleaded some more with him, wanting him to call an ambulance. "No Jan, I am not doing that, I love you, you know that." "I love you too Ronnie." I called Gene immediately, he was in New York, and I asked him to call Ron and convince him to go to the hospital.

While Gene was calling and talking to Ron, I ordered the wheelchair. I called back, and my niece answered, "We can't talk, the paramedics are working on Dad, he fell and he's not breathing." There was a snow storm going on, a bad one, I called Rudy and said I had to get to the hospital. He was far out in Indiana getting his girlfriend out of a ditch, and Michael said Mom, come to me, go twenty miles an hour, it will be quicker than If I go get you and I will take you to the hospital. I started out, the only car on the road. I got to Michael's and was switching seats so he could drive, when I got the call that my Ronnie was gone. I just fell to my knees in the snow and cried. Michael and I got to the hospital and my brother was still warm. I kissed him, and all of our family, all of us with our hearts breaking, tried to comfort each other. Losing Ronnie was a tremendous loss. March 5, at 10:14 p.m. was the last time I talked to my brother, and he told me he loved me.

I tell my children that when I die, they must never beat themselves up over any troubles they feel they may have caused me. Don't cry over harsh words said. I have never stayed angry with them longer than 20 minutes. The joy and love my family has given me far outweighs the bad that we have faced. I love every moment we have spent together. IT'S ALL GOOD.

Taken approximately 7 hours before my brother's death

Chapter 26:

A Little Help from My Friends

They say it takes a village...or no man is an island. I think about all the friends that have been there to help me through this life. People that are not in your daily life, but are "old school" and they remember where they came from. There is an old saying..."be respectful to the people you meet as you climb up the ladder, they are the same people you will see, on your way back down."

Lately I have had some strong messages from God. I have felt compelled to write this book. I'm going to be 66, and now I start writing a book? Why not a year ago, five years ago? I also find that my walk with God is escalating at a much quicker pace. Not by fear, my nephew phrased it best. We feel a calm resolution. I also feel the need to talk to those close to me about seeking a relationship with God. I get a lot of "Talk to the hand" looks, and some eye rolling on occasion. I understand that. Before I was saved, Tiffany started talking to me about her relationship with God, and how she was on fire with her faith. How did I feel about that? I said "don't you think you have gone a little over the top here? Aren't you getting carried away, and shouldn't you tone it down?" Janice, Janice, Janice…I sit here shaking my head as I think about those things I said to my daughter. I have so many favorite Bible verses. One comes to mind, when I think of a couple of my friends. When the Chosen One came into my life, I mentioned that I looked for strong role models. Men of character. Uncle Pete's no nonsense approach to doing a job well done. My neighbor Justin is the image of a Firefighter, and a guy that when asked for help says, "Sure, I can do that." Wally, ready to jump in, "Whatcha need Jan, how can I help you? The kid looks like he's doing a good job. Tell him I said to keep up the good work!" Jake, at the age of 21, when most people his age are self-centered, and they live by the "it's all about me" credo, telling me, "Sure, I would love to help make a difference in someone's life." Mike, a guy that lives such a clean life his nickname is "Choirboy." And Tim, the hot headed Irish Cop, who's middle name must be integrity. He was happy to enlighten the lad, about what WILL happen if you choose the wrong paths. Larry and Gene, who drummed it into my head that I must be ready to let the Chosen one fail, so that he can pick himself up, work through his problems and continue on again.

Several of these men are men of faith. I was talking to Pete about faith, and he turned to me and said "Jan, I do believe, do you know God saved my life when I was a kid? I know he saved me from drowning." Justin, talking to me about how he lives his life, "God first, Family second." And sharing several posts about his faith.

Jake, who was a part of the youth group I taught. "I do believe Jan, I have been disgruntled with churches in the past, but I do believe." And joining us, in prayer for a loved one in need. Of course Mike, Mike who attends church with his wife every week and frequently would ask the boy, "You pray don't you. Remember to pray kid!"

When I think of all of you, this Bible verse comes to mind. Matthew 25: 45 "And the King shall answer and say unto them, Verily I say unto you, Inasmuch as ye have done it unto one of the least of these my brethren, ye have done it unto me."

Our Pete

Firefighter Justin

Our Jake

Mike, a champion all the way around

Chapter 27:

Final Chapter

How many times have you heard, "It's my life, leave me alone or I'll do what I want." But it isn't our life. 1 Corinthians 6:19-20 says "What? Know ye not that your body is the temple of the Holy Ghost. (Which is) in you, which ye have of God, and ye are not your own."

I had a grandfather that committed suicide and my birth mother did too. I never knew either of them. I look back at my life, I am grateful for every moment. I am so glad that God chose me to be here. He gave me life.

My son Rudy was born, Dec 11th 1972. In 1973 my life took a dramatic nose dive. I couldn't cope, I saw a doctor, he prescribed a variety of medications to help me try to cope. I was in a bad situation, and I believed that since I made my bed, I should lay in it. I didn't ask for help from my family, and I spiraled downward. It was an effort just to get out of bed each day. I cried uncontrollably, until I didn't have any tears left. I could not find a way out of the dark hole I was in. If only I had opened my eyes, and my heart, and looked to God. I didn't ask him for anything. I don't think I outright rejected him, I think I just didn't have Faith in him, and that he felt I deserved a new chance in my life.

I voiced my sadness to a friend. He had no words to give me, to ease my pain. On a night when my husband was asleep, I took all my prescriptions the Doctor had given me. I had saved up the valium and other pills. I wrote a letter to my husband and I took every pill that I had. I then went and laid down on the floor next to my son's crib, where he was sleeping. I went into a drugged sleep. The phone was ringing, I heard from someone later on that it happened about 2 a.m. I never heard it. My friend was calling; he couldn't sleep and was worried about me. My friend expressed his fears to my husband, and he went looking for me, and he found me unresponsive, and called the ambulance. I don't remember much, I couldn't answer much, and they worked on me at the hospital and pumped my stomach. I was in a haze for three days, walking around like a zombie. Friends came to see me. One friend came to see me, and he later became my husband and Michael's father. He would come in the store where I worked, and he had heard the news "Janice tried to kill herself." He was friends with some of my friends and they brought him to the house. He talked to my mother, and told her. She didn't know him, but he was going to help me. He rescued me. I didn't have the strength to do anything, and he gave me advice and steered me to the right people that could help me. I will be ever grateful for him, caring enough to help, and for the structure he brought to my life. A ringing phone saved my life. I had taken more than enough medication to do the job. It wasn't really the phone, it was God and he intervened.

If I had been successful that day, I do not know how Rudy would have turned out, as I wouldn't have been there for him, he would have known as little about me, as I knew of my birth mother. Michael would have never been born. Tiffany would not have been taken into our family. Lily and London would not have been born. You see I got Tiffany a job at the company I worked for, and she met her husband through a coworker that threw a BBQ. So there would have been no marriage between Tiffany and Jeff. I would have never known my best friend's last wishes, nor would have ever met her; our paths would have never crossed. My friend and mentor that hired me would have never been a part of my life. There never would have been a first trip to the islands, let alone, countless trips after that. I would not have met Gene, or his sons. There would have been no blended family. Nor would I have met, Pete, Mike, Wally, Tim, Justin or Jake. The Chosen One and his Mrs. Foster would have never shown up in my life, and I doubt Tiffany would have found the boy either. I would not have been at my Father's side when he took his last breath, and I would not have become a born again Christian, baptized because I made the choice. I would not have known Michelle or Charlie. My brother would not have been a part of my life, as we did not spend a lot of time together when I was in my early twenties. Countless people, who have touched my life, and whose lives I have touched and tried to help, would not have factored in. I would never have spoken in tongues in deep prayer with my Savior. The list can go on and on.

It's like that movie A Wonderful Life, where they show what would have not happened if George Bailey was never born. God was with me at that time of my life when I didn't even know him. Jeremiah 1: 5 "Before I formed thee in the belly I knew thee, and before thou camest forth out of the womb I sanctified thee, and I ordained thee a prophet unto the nations." You are not your own master, you are God's child. Life is a precious gift, don't waste it, embrace it and love one another, as God so loved us.

One Year Later

I started this book last summer, and what a difference a year can make. So much has changed, some good, and some not so good.

Nick has found a terrific woman to share his life with, and we love her. Rudy is celebrating his second year with Shelby and loves being a Dad to little Adrianna. It's really cute to see him sending us pictures and videos, and he sold his precious car to buy a beautiful home for the three of them.

We recently had a family trip with all the little ones, and the children were all we hoped they would be. There were 13 of us, so I was pretty busy, but whenever Gene would play in the water with the grandchildren, I would stop what I was doing and take photographs in my mind. I couldn't go out in the sun, as I had some bouts with skin cancer, but I love those memory pictures of those moments that are so precious. We also were pretty proud of ourselves that we still "had it" when it came to the ability to enjoy them, and know that they were enjoying us back.

Lily is taking a break from dancing, as she wants to try track, and she runs like the wind. We will revisit dancing in the future, as she has the talent, but Lily has many talents, and she also is trying to teach herself piano by ear. Lily and our London are strong in their faith of our Lord Jesus. London is just filled with her love of God. Whenever I tell the two of them I love them, they always remind me that I have to love Jesus more. Lily is doing her best to convert Papa Gene.

London is five now, and recently she was doing a chalk drawing in her driveway. The picture was of a person and clouds, and the sun, and numbers. Jeff, her father, asked her what it was supposed to be. "It's Jesus Daddy. He is coming out of the heavens and the numbers are the days before he gets here!" WOW!!! I related the story to Rudy, and he immediately asked me "HOW MANY DAYS DID SHE PUT IN THE PICTURE?!" I told him "It doesn't work that way son."

Jeff and Tiffany attend a church in their neighborhood; however, the girls come to church with me sometimes on Thursday nights and for Vacation Bible School, at least when we can pry London away from Mom. My daughter and son in law both realize how important it is for the girls to be around God's people, and to form friendships with children that are brought up in homes that put God first.

I just shake my head and marvel, how my darling daughter Tiffany was once homeless, and I am always thanking God for putting that door in front of me and giving me the courage to go through it. She has given me so much.

The Chosen one passed his Fire Department and EMS courses, and then started backing away from the idea of having a career with the Fire Department. He was half way to a Fire Science degree when he announced to Jake and me that he wanted to leave college and join the Marines. Regardless of how much we admire and appreciate our servicemen and women, those words still strike fear in the hearts of parents and grandparents. Jake and I were no exception. We tried to talk him into staying in school, but we also knew he was trying to grow up. He wanted to take charge and if he failed, pick up and try again. We had some tense moments and situations, but I hope he will get back on track and is supposed to enlist in the fall. Jake, ever the loyal friend insisted that he will go with to the recruiter to make sure Justin "reads all the fine print" and understands everything. People ask me if I am disappointed that he walked away from a great career. I tell them that I hope he won't regret it some day; however, it is hard for me to be sad or unhappy when I see him reaching out to God.

We had one of those nights when sadness and fear can take hold, and he opened up and told me that he feels such a struggle for his life. He has been hanging with the wrong crowd, and I told him I was asking God to remove those people from his life. This was a whole new concept to me. I knew that you asked God to help and heal, but I never realized you can "pray things away." That you can rebuke things that are wrong. Renee from church explained it to me. "You can ask God to remove people from his life if they are not going to build him up, or if he is not going to bring them to God, and you pray for God's people to reach out to him." So I prayed and prayed. I told the Chosen One I was doing this, and everything came to a head one night when he opened up to me. "Munner, you have to stop praying people away, I don't have any friends anymore." "Well Grandson, I am going to keep praying that prayer, and I will ask God to send his people to reach out to you. What he said next was what I was waiting to hear. "I feel there is this battle going on over me, and that God is pulling me one way, and Satan the other. Please pray for me, and take me to my Mom right now, and have her pray too." It was almost 1 a.m. but we jumped in the car and woke Mrs. Foster, and the three of us prayed and prayed hard. It was such a Holy moment, and after I left to go home, he asked her to pray over him again and she did. He has his ups and downs. The boy is too darn good looking for his own good, and he doesn't have to look for women, they find him. The spirit is willing but the flesh is weak. One day while we were driving he was looking out the window checking out girls. He suddenly turned his head back in, and said, I don't want to look at the girl over there like that. I said "What do you mean?" He said I can tell by the way she is dressed that she is a Christian and I respect those girls. I never want to look at them with the wrong thoughts. He also said that in today's world, a girl will go home with you just because you bought her a hamburger. In fact, he had told me that girls have propositioned him the first time he met them. People are living in the flesh and not in the Spirit.

More and more it is a do whatever you feel like society, and sadly, it will only worsen. The world is a tough place for the young these days, and it's a tough place for the old too. Pastor told us not to be dismayed, as the only glimpse of Hell we will see is on this Earth, and that Jesus has many wonderful things in store when he comes to redeem his people and throw Satan in that pit. Sometimes my grandson comes for a Bible study; however, he tries to avoid church, and it was a blessing that he was there for the 60th anniversary of our Church. The Spirit is willing but the flesh is weak. When we go through trials and tribulations we STAND; we stand in our Faith and trust in our Lord. And we need to reach out more than ever. There are so many souls out there, and we cannot just sit on our hands. It is important for the world to understand who we are and what we are. We believe that the only Savior is Jesus, the only one true God. We believe that we find redemption through him. He died on the cross for us and he forgives our sins. We believe in water baptism at the age when you can comprehend that you are renouncing Satan, and that you are giving your life to Christ, and we baptize in Jesus' name. We believe in the Holy Ghost and the speaking in tongues, a wonderful gift from God that is mentioned so often in the Bible. Though there is much turmoil in our lives right now, I am in a wonderful place with God. In the last days, families will be torn, and children will turn against their parents, but we wait for our Savior to set things right. My prayer and my worship have intensified. Attending services is such a joy, and I cannot describe the elation I feel that God has blessed me with his gift of speaking in a language that only he understands. I do not have the gift of interpretation, but it is as real as the air we breathe. Lily, Michelle, Tiffany and the Chosen one have all been beside me at one time or another when it has happened; and it is there for the asking. God wants to bless you with this gift. When I am praying out loud, praising him, and it is him and I at that moment, it happens. It intertwines with my speech, and sometimes it is just a few seconds, and other times longer, but it is the closest and most spiritual thing I have ever experienced. I hope that anyone that reads this book will seek God and give themselves to our Savior and receive this gift. My husband and our sons are not saved, but I pray continually that they will be. God can do it all. In my past I believed in God. I was baptized in Jesus name ten years ago. My walk with him gets better every day.

The world is changing rapidly and I have not heard anyone say things are getting better. People are worried about ISIS, climate change, crime, the economy, GMO engineering, you name it. They want a feel good religion. They don't want to follow God's teachings and his word. Recently, someone I know and love told me I was a hater. They said this because I did not condone marriage between two people of the same sex. I am not a hater, I love people, and I have gay friends, BUT I CANNOT REWRITE THE BIBLE, and I cannot worry about their sin because I need to concentrate on MY sins and work on MYSELF. I am not here to judge anyone. I will not try to fit in political correctness and be accepting of everything. I will NOT pass judgement on others, but I MUST stand up for my FAITH and my beliefs. I can honestly say I do not hate anyone, and pray for all. There are plenty of churches that are bending to the desires of the people, and are only taking bits and pieces of the Bible, and disregarding the rest. We will not do that. We are standing on HIS WORD, and the world does not like that. The flesh fights the spirit, we need to draw closer to God, and Satan will do all he can to put stumbling blocks in your path. I constantly rebuke him, and refuse to let him steal my joy that God has given me. I am blessed and I am God's child.

Lastly, what is holding you back? If you say nothing, that you have found Jesus, then I say PRAISE GOD. If you haven't found him, then start looking. "Seek and Ye shall find" he is giving you this time to come to him, and the time is growing short. We don't know how much time we have been promised on this earth, and so I close with this final message...Jesus is coming to reclaim his people, please be one of them.

Lily performing in a showcase

Collin

Lorelei

Adrianna

Picture taken 2015 on trip with Papa Gene and I

We love them so much

Tiffany and London 2014

London's chalk drawing of Jesus' return

Mom, our GG today

2015 Munner, Lily and London

Rudy's Letter

I never sent you the letter I wrote...I think you could probably use it today.

Momma, I wanted to write you. I listened to a song. The Rain Song. I've heard it hundreds of times, but not like this. I started thinking of you. All I could think of was when I was small, when we lived by Cal Park. I have vivid memories of us from then, from before Michael was born.

I think of the simple things you used to share with me. I looked at the world so different then. We would look at a dandelion together, the grass, moths and butterflies. I find myself doing these things with little London, showing her the things around her. I thought about when we would walk together in the park and I would try to climb the monkey bars. They were so old most of the paint was always worn off. Then we would get a drink from the concrete water fountains they had. I remember always looking back at our tall apartment building from the back as we would walk over the train tracks to the park. You have no idea how much I think of those days we would spend at the rocket slide together.

This song is so beautiful I can feel those warm summer days on the East Side with you, when I listen to him singing. The world will never be like that again.

I would sit on the floor looking at all of our record albums with you…on our red shag carpet. When I would be alone, I would lie upside down in our beanbag chair and stare at my reflection in the mirrored base. I think about the walks we would take in the neighborhood, and I would always pay close attention to the concrete…to the tiny pebbles that were embedded in it.

Most of the houses had those grey rough feeling wall tiles. I remember you would give me a bath in our pink bathroom. You would pour my pink Mr. Bubble bubble bath in it. Then I would also have my dinosaur bubble container to play with. I can smell the soap to this day.

You have taught me so many things. Things that are so important, about how to treat other people. You get happy when I give a homeless person money, but this I learned from you.

We had that poor boy in our neighborhood who was missing a leg, and you would call him over and give him money. I learned sorrow, generosity, and compassion from you at a very young age. Things that have carried with me all my life. I would feel so sad thinking about that boy for a long time. I never once made fun of a kid at school for being overweight, and if someone was slow, I would be nice to them and treat them as a friend.

Later in life I became a troubled person. Things took me over, and I can't even begin to tell you how dark my life was. I hit absolute bottom. I was not around for you and I was not around for my dad when Grandpa Bubbles died. I can't imagine how it feels to have something you love so much fall apart in front of you. I look at Lily and London and wonder what will become of them...if they will ever ignore me, or ever turn to horrible things like I have. I will probably never know what it feel like to be a parent, but I do know what it feels like to have let one down. You never gave up on me, and your love saved me. I may be the most forgetful person in the world, but have been blessed with an amazing long term memory. Sometimes I feel I can recall my entire childhood it seems. I wish I could write out every single memory I have of us together, so I could really show you how important you are and always were to me, and how much I love and adore you more than anything I ever will in my entire life.

You always went beyond to do all of the little things for us. We loved Christmas so much together. Do you remember when we would get all the Christmas decorations out and decorate the basement together? There was always a smell of candles in the air, it smelled like Christmas. I remember looking at the dove candle you would always light, it was burning and the wax was all melted to a liquid around the flame...when I touched it, it was so hot, but then we looked at the wax cooling on my little finger and then peeled it off.

You and I would draw Christmas cards to send to everyone. I was amazed how you would take our skinny markers and draw the Christmas trees and make the little ornaments on each one. Christmas was always such a special time for us. We both have been blessed with a gift of a little girl named Lily. For you and I to both have this connection with this child, we know she is truly special. It is so strange how we can see this in her. We can see how when we are gone someday, that parts of us will still be living on with her. You and I can only feel this special connection we have, nobody else will ever know it, or understand, but it is in her. I look at her and she reminds me of what you must have been like when you were her age. I am truly amazed with her presence in our lives, and I am so grateful for Tiffany being able to give you this joy that I couldn't. I am overwhelmed and so happy you have these grandchildren.

I look at the world today and I realize how lucky I really am. I got to experience the last of the great times... when the world and society were just normal. I guess it's kind of the very end of what life in the 50s was like. We would walk to school, ride our bikes all night, play outside without worry. I am so happy I grew up before cell phones and computers. Kids today stare at a screen in their hands...you and I would point to the clouds together, sit in a field of grass and fly kites in the summer. Time seemed like it would never end...the days were so long. I am so happy you brought me into the world when you did. Things will never be like that again, you have no idea how happy it makes me feel to have lived during these times. The world has become a very evil place; I hope you understand I do not want to bring a child into it.

One of the hardest days in my life was recently. When I listened to you stand in front of Uncle Ron's casket and tell us your stories and the feelings you had for him, it tore me apart to see you in so much sorrow. You will never know what it was like for me to hear you say that you will always be alone now without him. I've never cried so much. I am crying right now. I have never in my life been so sorry for you and helpless inside. I want you to know that when you are gone someday, that would be my exact feeling...alone for the rest of my life. I have great fear in losing something so important to me, someone who is my everything.

I promise you this...you will never be alone.

I love you.

Rudy.

This Morning

This morning, September 13 2015, God sent me a message in a dream. No there wasn't a booming voice in my ears saying, "JANICE THIS IS GOD! ARE YOU LISTENING?" It just came as a gentle reminder, a reminder that I had forgotten to add a beautiful miracle he gave me.

I was in REM, Rapid Eye Movement, sleep where you dream right before you wake up. My father appearing in my dream and giving me a message for Bobby was during that type of sleep.

After the abortion, I had a tubal ligation. It was recommended that I don't have any more children. I desperately wanted another child, but I went through the procedure and my childbearing days were over.

This morning, God reminded me of the prayers he answered. The vision in that dream was not so much a picture, but a beautiful colorful thought. Here's what God showed me, "You forgot that after you could bear no more children, that I gave you a miracle. I sent you Tiffany." I suddenly awoke and started searching events in my memories, and YES! Tiffany came into my life several months after I had the surgery. My personal gift from God was my daughter, and he gave her to me even though I have aborted a baby in the past, and he forgave too.

After the dream and revelation of this memory, I thanked him. My friends, start thanking him! When you pray and ask for what you need, don't be like the child tugging on her mother's coat trying to get attention. HE KNOWS WHAT YOU NEED ALREADY. START THANKING HIM, START BELIEVING IN HIS BLESSING, AND HAVE FAITH. We don't need to keep reminding him of what we need the way we remind a teenager to make his bed. HAVE FAITH, THANK HIM, AND BELIEVE!

CPSIA information can be obtained
at www.ICGtesting.com
Printed in the USA
LVOW02s1952021115

460794LV00006B/18/P